B53 068

THE WEDDING FAIRY'S
BIG DAY
BREAKDOWN
PLANNING FOR AN UNFORGETTABLE CELEBRATION

OAK TREE PRESS

George Watts

First published worldwide in 2013 by Oak Tree Press
An imprint of Andrews UK Limited
The Hat Factory
Bute Street
Luton, LU1 2EY

www.andrewsuk.com

Cover Design by Nick Tiseo

Printed and bound by CPI Group (UK) Ltd
Croydon, CR0 4YY

Contents

massive thank you to both Andrews UK and SLM Management who have made this book possible. I have had the pleasure of working with some amazing suppliers over the last few years and thank you all for your creativity that I have been lucky enough to share with the World. And of course all my family and friends who constantly put up with me talking cakes, flowers and dresses – thanks y'all.

About George

Imagery by D B Photography Sussex

Described by the UK's leading wedding website *confetti.co.uk* as an internet sensation, George is now recognised as a leading voice on all things connected to the biggest day of your life! Having spent 2 years reporting for *Wedding TV* on everything linked to the World of Holy Matrimony, George is now putting pen to paper so he can share all his top tips of the trade and little black book of knowledge to make any celebration positively A-List. With a million hits and counting on *YouTube* alone, George - The UK's ultimate Wedding Fairy, knows the perfect recipe for creating a truly spectacular big day and this guide is certainly no exception. Indeed, his attempt at transforming into a sophisticated Burlesque dancer - all in the name of hen parties of course, has attracted over 300,000 viewers on YouTube alone – now that's commitment for you! Add into the mix appearances on *BBC Radio, Sky, The Good Food Channel, The Wright Stuff on FIVE* - discussing a spectrum of topics related to weddings, and you have most definitely arrived at the right place for all the expert inspiration you need to make your role at the Ceremony simply sensational!

On top of all this, George is a regular contributor to a range of National Magazines such as *Perfect Weddings* plus, he also manages a personal consultancy offering couples one to one support and planning services for their big day. In 2011 George hit the screens stateside as the official Wedding Expert for *Discovery TLC's* super glam coverage of The Royal Wedding. A global audience of 22million watched as George commented on proceedings live from ITV studios in central London, along with fellow guests including the legendary Ivana Trump and a-list movie star Rupert Everett. George also hosted a Royal banquet feature for TLC during their Royal Wedding countdown show on the eve of the big event itself with a global audience of nearly 100 million across 60 Countries Worldwide. As well as all this he has contributed to *Hollywood daily's in LA*, the outrageous *50 Greatest Wedding Shockers for* E4, the *Market Kitchen Royal Wedding specials with Penny Smith* for The Good Food Channel and *The Alan Titchmarsh Show* for ITV1.

George is also creator and founder of *National Wedding Day* - an annual event that gives couples globally a chance to rejoice and re-live the most sensational day of their life!

It's time to sprinkle a little love across the Nation...

www.theweddingfairy.tv
The destination for planning a perfect Wedding.

When you wish upon a star

Welcome love disciples, to the most important read of your life! Yes the rollercoaster ride to your aisle of Holy Matrimony starts right here and what a journey it will be. The waiting is over, the champagne is on ice and a lucky Prince or Princess Charming is waiting in the wings for your Grande entrance. No more shall one need to dine alone on a sweaty boil in the bag, for the banquet of love awaits my darlings and no matter what the budget, this book will give all the detail needed to inspire, delight and steer you every step of the way. More importantly, it really doesn't matter what style of wedding or civil ceremony you are planning, this guide is all about arming you with the fundamentals to plan a sensational day. Oh yes Ladies and Gents - the gooseberry days are officially over!

From this moment on, I, George Watts your Official Wedding Fairy do solemnly swear that you shall go to the ball and shine beyond Cinderella's wildest dreams. This is your chance to sparkle like a superstar so soak it up girlfriend. As of this very second, I want you to feel magical from the inside out and all I ask in return is that you walk with an open mind and be prepared to try anything once! Every day I meet so many brides-to-be who have their big day all mapped out from the word go and it really stifles their creativity and individual journey. Like a dress, or a new person you meet, it is often those things we think won't fit or we won't like that turn into our best friends. Treat your wedding the same and trust me, the stress levels will stay in neutral and never shall you turn into a Bridezilla!

This is an important time to both mentally and physically prepare yourselves for the road ahead whilst basking in the euphoria of finding Mr or Mrs Right. So, before we move forward why not take a second to look back and reflect on that incredible moment when you said yes or (if you were brave enough) popped the magical question yourself. It might have been a flash of comedy genius or the most romantic two minutes of your life? Every occasion, however odd is always perfect. During my career I have heard everything from a bit of bling inside a bad-boy Big Mac to a live public address at the local bingo hall. Who could forget the dreamy engagement of David and Victoria Beckham? The great man himself simply took his beau to a local restaurant and went down on one knee. A simple yet elegant proposal that worked a treat! There is no right or wrong way to make that most decent of proposals nor is it ever a disaster – every I do has its own unique and memorable story to tell. So, when you are having a moment of mild hysteria over a dodgy dress fitting or the wedding car hasn't turned up on time, just remind yourself of what this journey is really all about. This fairytale goes way beyond just hair and make-up; it's about sealing the deal with your other half and making your own dream a reality. Keep things in perspective and trust me, this process will be all pleasure and no chore. All you need is love as they say!

The next few pages are literally all about you, so pop yourself on the sofa, grab a bottle of something fizzy and enjoy every second. It really doesn't matter whether you have 1 month or 1 year to plan the day itself, each step is in chronological order so you can make it to the aisle on time no matter what schedule you are on! As in life, timing is of the essence and in the world of weddings; a schedule is a TOTAL MUST...

And finally, remember this particular fairytale has no rules or regulations set in stone. I want you to freestyle and stamp your own personality all over your big day without having to be censored. This book is not just about the technicalities of planning a wedding; it's also about making you feel a million dollars for the big day and beyond. Ladies and gents, say goodbye to singledom - the magic starts when you turn this page...

Let's get this show on the road my little love disciples!

Big Kiss

THE WEDDING FAIRY'S
BIG DAY
BREAKDOWN
PLANNING FOR AN UNFORGETTABLE CELEBRATION

Fairy toolkit

*R*ight troops before we head off to the chapel of love it's essential for us to pack my all important kit of tools to maximise pleasure and minimise pain. Every fairy has a wand of magic and a box of tricks up their sleeve and I am no different! Ladies and gents, this chapter is all about preserving and prospering through your journey...

Any bride or groom-to-be planning a wedding should consider this adventure an extended holiday or an extreme day trip minus the soggy sandwiches and eighties anorak. As many of us learnt from a young age, any decent Cub Scout, Brownie or in my case the very nautically themed Sea Cadet should be prepared for all eventualities. A wedding my friends, is no different. Forget compasses and home cooking badges though, I am talking serious kit here! Well actually, you will be pleased to hear I am not really talking about anything too serious. Just a few ways to save some memories, look the business to barter money saving deals and give yourself a few treats along the way!

So to start, we need a treasure chest to really kick this little adventure off with a bang! A cherished place to store all those pieces of the jigsaw that make your big day complete. Every snippet of detail (however insignificant it may seem at the time) is a golden nugget in conserving your journey together. Think of yourself as a mini Indiana Jones enshrining your own piece of history. Everything from the venue booking confirmation to your first dress fitting appointment card should be included. Funnily enough, it's those moments of insignificance that can often prove most powerful. I even have a wee memory box for this very book don't you know! Remember, any snippet of inspiration you pick up along the way - whether it be from a magazine or via the net, rip it out, print it and get it in the box!

Right next up, to go with this chest of treasure we need another vital piece of kit. What I hear you ask? Well troops, get out those trusty throw-aways or for you modern types the digital camera to get snap happy and capture every second of the fairy tale as it unfolds, with your very own *big day photo diary!* No wedding memory box is complete without one. I want the drunken moments at the engagement party, the euphoria of booking the venue and all the tears at the dress rehearsal... I am welling up just thinking about it! See what I mean?! The magic is happening in front of our very eyes already.

Ok, let's get serious team. Forget Sir Alan and Mr Branson, I want to ensure you look the part and talk the talk when you get down and dirty with your suppliers. Make sure you are armed with all the essential kit including calculator, notebook and pen or indeed some suitably modern 21st century equivalents. Remember, the wedding industry is predominantly managed by local suppliers, which means you can always barter for a better deal. Simply advise your budget and see what can be achieved. Sometimes when you mention the *W* word things can get a little bit pricey so, to stay on top of the game, you need to mean and look the business. If financial management is not necessarily your forte, make sure you have a trusted friend or family member at your side to play the role of *personal wedding planner*, which in many cases can get you a great deal from the off, as suppliers aim to impress and bag more business.

And finally, because you are totally gorgeous and deserve it, I want you to start popping a little poppy aside post haste to give yourself a delicious detox pre-wedding day. Choose from a totes heavenly oxygen facial or even a blissful Mani slash Pedicure - the list is endless! Every girl deserves the odd moment of personal pleasure and self- indulgence, so why not kick off pre-wedding. Not only will you look utterly fabulous, this little treat is perfect in helping you stay cool, calm and collected or, *in the zone* as my good friend Britney would say. Go for it Princess!

To add an additional touch of wonderment to this mini ritual, I always advise bringing in the traditional Terramundi money pot. I just love these little jars of joy that have been knocking about for over 2000 years. So what's the deal I hear you ask? Well, these are not just any old bog standard money pots my darlings, oh no, the Terramundi is a wedding wishing well and good luck charm for the big day itself. Once the first coin has been dropped inside the said pot, you must keep feeding it coins daily until it is full, upon which time it must be smashed whilst making a wish. All the cash inside can then be spent on something super deluxe just for you. It is also customary to replace each broken Terramundi pot with a new one, so you can continue wishing and treating yourself every few months. Screw the wedding girls, let's just spend it all on a-list oxygen facials instead! I am looking up 'Terramundi pots' online as we speak!

To recap then, we need a treasure chest to capture your voyage of love, a camera to get snap happy with, a splash of accessories that show you mean business, a beauty fund because you're worth it oh and the stamina of a horse!

Ok, let's do it! We are good to go!

The three fundamentals

*B*efore we really get going, it's important we cover these crucial points that totally underpin the world of wedding planning and will help take the stress out of your journey to the aisle of love right from the beginning...just think **BUDGET, PLAN AND LOOK -**

Money talks!

How much cash have you got to splash?! Calculate a running total and break down the costs for each element of your big day. Take out 10% of your overall budget to act as an emergency fund for any costs that may crop up along the way or, to top-up cash allocation for specific elements such as the cake and flowers. Ensure you clearly work out your spend per head for the wedding reception as this is one area that always causes a headache for most couples - especially if not considered in advance of any planning meeting. Remember, if you have all your figures prepped before you get together with suppliers they will know you mean business. Many couples like to do the maths on an excel spreadsheet to tally running totals, but personally I L O V E the free budget breakdown resource offered online via hitched.co.uk. When I discovered this service, I just knew it would be a lifesaver for so many couples needing an organised check list. Online registration takes a few minutes but trust me, it's so totally worth it to access this top admin tool. Check out the detail at www.hitched.co.uk

Big day Bible

An essential bit of kit for any wedding planner to be, *The Big Day Bible* is your personalised a-z checklist of what to do and when. From securing the venue to selecting the dress, a concise countdown of jobs-to-do, is a total must-have piece of kit for anyone planning a big day celebration. Investing time in this plan right from the off, guarantees to ease your overall journey to the aisle of love, whilst at the same time ensuring you have everything effectively in place ready for the wedding itself - without stress levels reaching boiling point. And by a total stroke of luck, the next section of this book - *your official wedding day countdown,* will act as a blueprint/ inspiration board for said BDB! More on this in the next section...

Get in the mood - for romance

Every wedding needs a clear style or theme to bind the celebration together and knowing where to start can be a challenging task. I know it's a bit of a cliché, but the best approach is to start with a blank canvas, so you can build a unique picture of your celebration organically. Do not stifle your creativity with too many set ideas right from the beginning, start with an open mind and see what evolves. The true genius of a person is often bubbling subconsciously... here's what to do:

Spend an afternoon grabbing a ton of wedding, food, home design and celebrity magazines highlighting your favourite dresses, interiors, menus and hairstyles. Rip out the pages you love and pop on a big board to create a montage of imagery. This we know in the business as a *mood board,* which you can then use to identify your favourite themes, styles and colour-ways to slowly build an overall concept for the wedding. This *mood board* is also really handy for taking to supplier sessions - especially the cake maker and florist, to inspire and steer their creativity.

And for those who prefer a more modern approach, remember www.pinterest.com is now one of the world's number one online sites to pick up inspirational wedding ideas. Build yourself a digital board via an Ipad or similar device and use this to take along to supplier sessions. Many of the National wedding magazines also have Pinterest boards now, so it's definitely a great place to start getting those creative juices flowing!

The wedding planning countdown

$\mathcal{T}$ime to get this show on the road party planners! Remember, I have laid out this quick-fire checklist in timeline format, but ultimately you just need to work through in the chronological order as listed - no matter what timeframe you are working within...

12 + Months
In the beginning

So, where do we start? Back to the budget of course! Let's re-cap. I cannot emphasise how important it is to seriously work out how much dosh you have to splash on your big day. I meet so many couples who don't do this from the off and 9 times out of 10, it ends in hideous disaster, with the wedding being more of a financial headache than a happy ever after. Remember, a fairytale does not have to cost a fortune. Utilise every talent available via your inner circle of family and friends. Make sure you tell anyone and everyone who will listen that you are tying the knot because someone somewhere will know a photographer, a hairdresser, a DJ or indeed anyone connected to the wedding industry that you might be able to negotiate a cheeky rate with. Everyone loves a good barter and you will be surprised how far you can stretch your cash in the W world by simply asking. The important bit is to pay all your invoices as they become due to stay ahead of the game. And finally, be subtle regarding any parental contributions, actually, who am I kidding, be subtle as a brick and get them to support in any which way they can!

Right planners, next up we need to think about that *big day bible*. Month by month I want to know what is going on and when it's happening! At this stage it's best to read through my breakdown as a whole and then you can extract and create your own bespoke version to meet your individual needs as you wish. It might be that this quick-guide works perfectly well as your blueprint, in which case you are totally good to go.

When considering said *big day bible* please also allow some 'you' time for rest and relaxation. Organise some 'non wedding' activities to do together with your partner each week in the months leading up to the big day. Even a trip to your local cinema will help take the edge off any natural anxiety or stress during the build-up. The planning process is not just about cakes and flowers - it's also about your well-being in what can be a very stressful period.

At this stage, the wedding date and selecting a venue is top dog priority. Once this is set everything else will fall into place. If you have a dream venue in mind, go visit the wedding coordinator and ask what can be achieved with your budget. Don't be afraid to ask! Hog-roasts and summer bbq's are all the rage at the moment and can often be much lighter on the budget compared to a traditional sit down meal. If you are not sure on a venue, pick out five in your local area and go from there (unless of course you are planning a destination wedding). Even if you don't like any of them, hopefully they will spark some ideas. Remember don't be shy, just give a few venues a try and be adventurous; think about finding a space that reflects you both as a couple. If you love the ocean why not go nautical or maybe a medieval banquet is more your thing?

12 + Months Checklist

- Set your big day budget (allowing 10% for overspending). It is a good idea to open a joint wedding account to monitor funds and expenditure.

- Discuss openly with immediate family who will be contributing to the wedding - it's important to sort such technicalities out at the very beginning of this process. If you feel uncomfortable asking a direct question, initially mention the budget as a passing comment to sow the seed as they say... that is if they don't mention it first! Tact and diplomacy is the name of the game here. It is also important to be understanding of individual financial circumstances.

- Finalise the wedding date - choose and book a venue for the ceremony and reception. For venue ideas in the UK visit www.weddingvenues.com or for weddings abroad visit www.weddings-abroad-guide.com

- Arrange a meeting with your priest, minister, rabbi or registrar to discuss dates and plans for the wedding (more on this in terms of timings within the Q&A section).

- Choose key members of your wedding party... chief bridesmaid, bridesmaids, bestman, ushers and pageboys alongside key family members.

- Pick out or design your save-the-dates cards, invites and thank you cards. Get inspired via my friends at www.hummingbirdcards.co.uk

- Make a decision about how many guests to invite to the ceremony/reception and begin making a guest list. Remember to allocate a reception budget and work out how much you can spend per head based on attendees. Cull where necessary! Plan a separate list for evening attendees as appropriate.

- Send save-the-date cards if your wedding is in peak season or taking place abroad. High street retailer Debenhams also offers a bespoke design service for wedding stationery visit www.debenhamsweddingstationery.com for more details.

9+ Months
Strike a pose!

Ok, 9 months is all about research, planning and booking. The bridesmaid outfits and *your dress* are priority numero uno. It's time to start thinking about your overall styling for the big day because Cinderella will go to the ball (past midnight hopefully) and look a billion glitzy dollars regardless of budget! Grab a ton of wedding dress images and stick them in a ma-hoosive scrap book for inspiration, take this along to your chosen dressmaker or store for inspiration... remember the Ipad if you are using Pinterest! Make sure you allow yourself a dressing up day with the girls and try on lots of dresses you might not even like the look of. Sometimes a girl can be surprised. Infact in my experience, it is always the dress we think won't work that does! Whatever you do, just remember that magical line, 'Fashions fade, style is eternal' - Yves Saint Laurent. What a God!

Lets talk more about - the dress

For many brides-to-be this is where the pressure really kicks in - unearthing the one! And I am not talking about your man! The hunt for a dream dress can often be a stressful affair and knowing where to start can be just as bad. Heading straight to your local bridal store can sometimes be a bit of a gamble and often means you settle without fully investigating all options. So, before commencing all that legwork, why not start on the sofa and check out my four fabulous online finds to get an idea of what might work for you. Yes, these little nuggets of gorgeousness are buzzing with bridal fashion, direct from the coolest catwalks on the planet and offer a stunning array of glitzy artisan accessories that you just won't find on any standard high street. We are talking A-list here people, but not necessarily with the A-list price tag! These little black books of fashion heaven are teaming with originality and are updated hourly to ensure you are kept abreast of what's hot and happening - literally as it happens! Here's my official run-down Ladies:

www.lovemydress.net - I just adore this site for sourcing super sassy accessories and discovering new designers most of us would never hear of otherwise!

www.weddinggowntown.com/blog - From Vera Wang to Valentino, if it's on the catwalk it's in wedding-gown-town! I love this blog for identifying new trends and pointing out upcoming styles for the season ahead.

www.bridechic.blogspot.com - A joyous homage to bridal fashion, with Bride Chic we also get some really fantastic out-of-the-box ideas and distinct styling themes - ideal if you are looking for a strong non-traditional big day look.

www.lovelybride.com/blog - And finally with Lovely Bride we uncover some edgy classics alongside a wonderful mix of real life weddings - perfect for seeing how a dress truly comes to life on the day itself.

9+ Months Countdown

- Book wedding insurance... Get the low-down via www.moneysupermarket.com/wedding-insurance

- Start researching dresses, shoes and accessories. Organise a mission-brides-dress-day with the girlies to check out a whole mix of bobby dazzlers... with a few glasses of bubbly thrown in simply for glamour purposes of course! Oh I feel a Wedding Fairy SOS coming on!

- Order invites and thank-you cards

- Finalise your gorgeous guest list

- Research local accommodation for out-of-town guests and start putting a list of options at varying budgets together to include in your invite.

- Consider putting together a fun wedding website to keep guests up-to-date with your plans or create a Facebook page to stay in touch. Visit www.mywedding.com/free-wedding-websites for ideas.

- Plan the honeymoon and consider booking now if you are travelling in peak season and don't forget to book time off work! For inspiration visit www.101honeymoons.co.uk

- Make a final decision on your dress/shoes and place your order - this is the super exciting bit when the whole W thing starts to become a reality...

- Pick out and order the bridesmaids dresses - J'adore www.maidstomeasure.com

- Put together your gift list and remember to include present ideas to suit all budgets. For an alternative to the traditional retail gift list, check out www.turquoiseholidays.co.uk. I love their interactive online wedding gift list that allows your guests to make a cash contribution to your honeymoon package or buy an experience to enjoy whilst you are there! An ideal option if you are already fully loaded with toasters and tea towels... anyone for a Margarita?

- Send out invites if your wedding is in peak season or to those who are coming from abroad (remember to put an RSVP date to save last minute chasing, include gift list details and wedding website link as appropriate). Remember your wedding day invite should also be suitably styled to reflect your overall theme for the big day, so your guests get a clear understanding on the tone, look and formality of the wedding.

6+ Months
Let's get ready to rumble!

Oh yes, this is it! With only 6 months to go, you need to stop researching and start making some decisions quick sharp. The past few months have been spent putting in the ground work for your dream day and now you have to start making it a reality. Live by your *big day bible* and start spending! Remember to discuss payment procedures with any potential supplier in advance of booking. Some might have better deals than others, therefore making your final decision a little easier! Make sure you get all agreements in writing.

In a few months time, everything is going to slot into place - I am hysterical just writing about it!

6+ Months Countdown

- Send out invites NOW if you haven't already

- Start researching and book your photographer (don't forget to look up family and friends who might be keen amateurs to get on-board for this role... great for the budget!), finalise menu with your caterers, start planning with your chosen florist and book a cake-maker (see my inspiration chapter later in the book).

- Start to look at the process of changing your name on legal documents; get together all necessary paper work...

- Here's a link to a great UK online resource that outlines all the key factors to consider: www.weddingguideuk.com/articles/legal/changingnamemarriage.asp. If you want to change your name on a passport for your honeymoon, you need to allow plenty of time to action this (6-8weeks) and you also need to get your minister or registrar to sign the passport form. Check out all legalities relevant to your home Country.

- Your Fiancé should now start looking at outfits for himself and his key attendants - bestman/ushers/Father of the Bride etc. The team at www.hugharris.co.uk offers a stand out collection.

- Sit down with bridesmaids to delegate jobs. Traditionally ones chief bridesmaid will be tasked with planning the hen party and support in the overall wedding planning process where needed. Of course their main role is in helping to choose the dress and assisting the bride in getting ready on the wedding day itself. Do you want a bridal shower? If so, your chief bridesmaid might want to get planning this for you too!

- Make sure your fiancé orders his wedding day outfit!

- Book your honeymoon if you haven't already!

- Confirm the order for your ceremony and decide on plans for the service, readings and music (If you are getting married in a church you will need to talk to the minister and organist directly about the choice of music). The individual registrar or religious centre you have chosen to marry in will be able to provide a template for the ceremonies structure/legal regulations to guide you.

- The important bit - discuss potential ideas or things you would like to do for the stag and hen parties with maid of honor and best man. Visit www.gohen.co.uk and www.gostag. co.uk for some serious inspiration!

3+ Months
Time to get this party started!

Well girls, the last 9 months of planning and research all comes into play right now as you lay down your cards and splash the last of your cash. Now is the time when your big day should really start taking shape. It's exciting times... wedding rings, entertainment and dress fittings - the list is endless! This month has the potential to be rather hectic, so make sure you set aside some quality R&R time to prevent any potential stress attack! Whatever the situ, just remember to stay calm and carry on with the countdown!

Now sadly we are not all naturally gifted with being super organised, so if you do feel things are getting a little out of control and your plan is not going to plan as they say, make sure you do to turn to a family member or friend for support. We all have that one person in our lives who loves to get out their a-z checklist at any given opportunity, so make sure you get them on board if needs be. There is still lots of time left so ultimately *don't panic*. The aisle is in sight now I promise!

3+ Months Countdown

- Book your wedding night hotel if not at same venue. Check out www.mrandmrssmith.com for some serious boutique action!

- Pick out your blingtastic wedding rings! Take a look at www. hatton-garden.net for the very best from this World Famous jewellery and diamond centre in London.

- Time for another dress fitting!

- Book in your wedding day rehearsal, ideally a few days before the actual wedding.

- Decide on the entertainment for your wedding - book a band or DJ. For a great mix of live music ideas visit www. bandsforhire.co.uk. And if you are on the look-out for a harpist, toastmaster, circus performer or even a bagpiper visit www.alivenetwork.com!

- Book that all important wedding day transport.

- Make any final adjustments to your menu with the caterers. Remember to personalise! What is your ultimate 3 course dinner...?

- Hire a make-up artist and hairdresser if you are not doing your own. Make sure you have a few trial runs to figure out a look you are happy with. If you are planning your own hair and make-up start experimenting with styles now.

- Run through everything with your fiancé to make sure he/she has organised everything they were supposed to... attendant's outfits, wedding gifts, rings, transport and any other specific duties assigned for the big day.

- Find out if you need visas or inoculations for your honeymoon.

- The Best man and Chief bridesmaid must now organise and book your stag and hen parties - ensuring they notify all hens and stags of arrangements and date. If you are planning a weekend break, I would give a 4-6month lead-time. The longer people have to prepare, save cash and pop the date in their diaries the better.

2+ Months
This is it!

With just 2 months to go, it's time to have some fun people! Hopefully the nitty gritty details are now well under control and you can start thinking sexy undies and shopping with the girls. This is a time for you and your partner to really start enjoying the build-up. Practice your vows in bed, rehearse the wedding ceremony and wash it all down with a bottle or two of your favourite vino! The latter will definitely help with those pre-wedding day nerves, but defo don't binge drink... think of your skin!

At this stage, I would also have another read through of this countdown to ensure your *big day bible* is going to plan and all the key elements have been checked off... just for peace of mind of course.

2+ Months Countdown

- Chase any guests who have not RSVP'd

- Start writing personalised vows and start considering content of speeches

- Take this opportunity to buy some gifts for the wedding party and all those who have supported your journey.

- Now is also a good time to purchase some wedding favours for your guests to enjoy at the reception. For a mix of fabulous ideas visit www.favourfairy.co.uk and for an old-skool trip down memory lane click www.lovehearts.com

- Shop for decorations (more on this in my little black book coming up later in the book)

- Give your caterers/venue a final number of guests and decide on a seating plan if you are having one.

- Buy your honeymoon outfits and all the necessary essentials to go with. Whilst on that subject, don't forget your bridal underwear for the big day itself. For some seriously sassy numbers visit the motherland of all undie-creations www.agentprovocateur.co.uk/bridal

1 Month
Let's get this gig on the road!

It's not unusual for a spot of anxiety to start kicking-in at this point, with the big day just around the corner and almost a reality. A splash of adrenaline is never a bad thing. Now is the time when you both need to stand firm as a team and be there to support each other. Keep sight of how you felt 11 months ago and how magical you will feel on the wedding day itself. If you start tensing up over minor details, just stop and imagine how incredible it's going to feel when you finally say *I do*. That special moment will help keep things in perspective. Grab that box of tissues girls - I feel a ceremony coming on!

1+ Month Countdown

- Have a final trial run with hair and makeup or, if you are doing your own make sure you are happy with the look you have decided on.

- Go back for a final dress fitting and try on the entire planned outfit - dress, shoes, underwear, veil/tiara and accessories. Rock it girl!

- Prepare place cards and menus for the tables - if not already organised during the earlier stages, as part of your overall stationery order.

- Book your wedding day transport if you haven't already.

- Start wearing-in your shoes at home, so they feel comfortable for the day itself (only on carpet so as not to ruin them).

- Make sure your fiancé has finished his vows/speeches. My eBook 50 top tips for giving the best best mans speech ever will make a perfect last minute gift for the best man to read through! And for general overall advice on speeches and much more for the groom, bestman and Father of the Bride visit www.iamstaggered.com

- Buy a guest book for all your friends and family to sign on the day.

- Pick a stunning going-away outfit! Check out some delicious designs via my friends at www.littleblackdress.co.uk

- Make sure you have your something old, new, borrowed, and blue for good luck!

1 Week
I'm so excited and I just can't hide it!

One week to go....STAY CALM. There may well be a last minute crisis, but if you remember everything from the last 12 months of planning you will be just fine. Where there is a will there is a way - truest saying my Mother ever taught me!

- Pick up your dress if you haven't already

- Pack for your honeymoon - don't forget the passport!

- Make sure you have purchased your holiday insurance and currency

- Speak with key suppliers - venue, caterers, florist, cake-maker and band to re-confirm booking details so you are not panicking the day before

- Plan and host a rehearsal dinner for immediate family and key wedding party (optional).

- Make sure your fiancé has an appointment to have his hair cut and is prepped with some serious grooming apparatus for the big day itself! Check out www.meetthebulldog.com for manly ideas.

- Plan out a schedule for the day itself based on timings for the ceremony and reception, just so every member of your key wedding party knows where they need to be and when. Make sure you allow yourself plenty of time to get ready in the morning and your driver allows enough time to get you to the service on time - ish! A little lateness is clearly tradition!

- Enjoy your hen and stag nights if you haven't already!

1 Day to go
I am getting married in the morning!

Just soak up every moment from now on because this day is all yours. Go with the flow and let everything simply fall into place. Enjoy a champers breakfast and make sure your nearest and dearest pamper you big time. Good luck for tomorrow...

1 Day to Go Countdown

- Have a big glass of wine and relax - here's to the ceremony!

And there's still more to come
don't forget the honeymoon!

Phew! And Relax

The week after the wedding

*P*ost honeymoon make sure all suppliers have been paid as agreed and anything hired has been returned. Send out all your thank you cards (including suppliers - you might need them again for the christening!) and organise a wedding night for all the key members of your big day to enjoy drinks, the wedding video and a few honeymoon snaps! If you haven't already changed all your legal documents you should also start that process.

Right, that's it! All I can say now is best of luck and enjoy every minute of your new beginning...

The Wedding Fairy's essential planning questions answered

I'm worried about the weather spoiling my wedding. Any tips on making my wedding weather proof!?

Right, first of all don't panic! Sadly even I, your devoted Wedding Fairy cannot control the weather but, like any decent wedding planner would advise - it's always essential to think ahead and plan for every eventuality.

Immediately of course the seasons come to mind, so consider carefully the time of year you want to get wed. Summer is of course your safest bet, but generally the most expensive. Personally, I love a delicious winter wedding. Yes it will be a bit chilly but, we often experience clear, sunny days (especially in the UK) at this time of year and it is always super romantic. A candlelit space is always dreamy, just pop on your feathered bolero and you are good to go!

On a serious note though, make sure your venue has alternative inside-spaces available should you need them for photos/drinks reception etc that might have been planned for an open-air space and ensure your chief bridesmaid always has instant access to an uber-glam brolly to shield you from any potential downpour. If you are getting wed abroad, make sure you also check average weather conditions before you book and consider your outfit carefully. If you are marrying in a humid climate, you need to ensure you dress appropriately in a light flowing number. A sweaty bride is a total no no!

Legal questions: How far in advance do I have to get my banns read out and notify the registrar?

If holding a traditional religious ceremony, the Banns need to be read out in your local parish church at least three Sundays before the big day itself and usually there is no need to involve your local registry office. For a civil marriage ceremony, your local registry office will generally take around 21 days to process and publish your license. Thankfully, doing a Britney by tying the knot on a whim - whilst severely intoxicated *Vegas style,* is currently illegal in the UK. No regrets in the morning for you my darlings!

If you have a specific religious ceremony in mind, it's always best to check with the individual centre concerned (at the beginning of your planning process) to find out any particular procedures/ codes of practice. Again, if outside the UK check relevant laws for your Country.

What would help make my wedding personal?

Think about your interests and passions as a couple and build those into your big day. It might be that you have a specific theme in mind, or maybe you could just add-in some subtle touches together such as; selecting your favourite flowers for the bouquet or personalising the reception menu - maybe inspired by your first dinner date?! Think about the demographics of your big day and any regional specialities. Are there local customs, traditions, or food produce that you can tap into to make your wedding day unique? Are you both mad film buffs and want to theme the whole day with a touch of Hollywood old school glamour? It might be that you are addicted sky-divers, in which case the sky's quite literally the limit! Be original and inventive at every opportunity, focusing primarily on the things you love and how you can integrate into the wedding.

Any tips for making my guests feel special/appreciated?

Personalise, personalise and personalise your wedding some more, oh and make sure you work that room! Remember, it's all about adding your individual character to each element of the celebration... cakes, flowers, dresses and all the big day regalia!

How to keep children and flower boys/girls occupied at the ceremony/reception?

A fun pack of goodies including games and colouring apparatus is always a good way to keep the little ones entertained during the wedding breakfast. Always check to see what additional services your venue can offer if you have a troop of little ones - a children's entertainer always goes down a treat. Why not try and allocate this task to a close friend or family member to save on paying out for a pro - especially if you focus around hosting a mini sports day event... I know a few clowns who would defo be up for the job!! Traditional pursuits such as the 'egg and spoon race' are highly entertaining when you get the adult guests involved too!

What are the most important questions to ask?

Rule number 1 - ask a supplier whatever is on your mind and don't be afraid to say what you think. If you are not happy with something, don't let it eat you away internally - this is your moment so make sure your opinions are heard...

The minister
Ensure your chosen minister guides you through *your* ceremony - clearly, from beginning to end so you can think about and add in all those personal little touches to make the day your own. Remember, many vicars, priests and registrars are performing ceremonies on a regular basis, so it's important not to be just another day.

Clarify where photographs can be taken, if confetti can be thrown outside the venue and ensure any additions to the service, such as music or readings are agreed at the rehearsal stage and not on the day itself!

The reception venue

Talk budget budget budget! Make sure you unearth *all* the venue costs with your event planner during the initial stages and get everything in writing... hidden costs have a way of rearing their ugly head as the wedding nears if you are not careful. Workout a total spend per head so you can keep on track with your budget, ensuring proceedings do not spiral out of control. Do not be tempted by any extras if you have not got the cash to splash! Trust me - it will only stress you out more in the end. Also, make sure you establish whether the venue will be exclusively yours for the whole day or not. Some venues will host more than one wedding at a time, which can be a problem for many brides-to-be.

The photographer

Find out exactly what your package includes in terms of on the day shooting and prints/electric images post wedding. Many couples are left disappointed by all the extra costs involved in producing the wedding day photo album, so make sure you know what you're getting before booking! This is a key rule with all suppliers in general. Also, in terms of imagery, are you looking to catch the day in a light documentary/reportage style or more formal portrait - perhaps a mix of both? Ask your photographer to take you through all the options/ packages available and request references from previous clients.

The band/DJ
It's all about the music people! Get that set list signed off and ask a family member or a trusted source to attend the venue sound check, just to make sure Aunt Bessie isn't going to be blown out the fire exit by extreme air guitar action!

The wedding transport
Organisation is the name of the game here people. Make sure your chosen supplier puts everything in writing with regards to their terms of contract and total costs for the period of hire. Ensure they allow for delays (at least 45mins either side of the ceremony), as generally a modern vehicle would be used for more than one ceremony per day. Vintage cars usually only operate one maybe two weddings in a day, but are obviously more expensive. Get your route plan confirmed in writing and ensure your driver will be armed with an umbrella and blankets to guard the bottom of your dress - just in case of a mini downpour, whilst stepping out of said vehicle. Most importantly, is champagne included?!

The florist
Maximise your florist's skills by arriving to your first consultation with a scrapbook of images, pulled from a range of trend driven magazines to reflect your individual style and look. Give each of your experts as much inspiration as possible. In my experience this is a real help for the florist in particular and means they can spend more time on creating and less of your cash thinking! Push your floral budget to the max by also ensuring your supplier uses local buds of the season.

The cake maker

When it comes to the baking action try and satisfy all your guest's sweet fantasies by serving two or three fillings - sadly fruit cake is not as popular as it once was! Get tasting and sampling post haste, ensuring all is washed down with a hefty glass of champers in practice for ones toast!

Alternatively, you could be super brave by going DIY and making the cake yourself or by holding a *big day bake off* with prizes for the best taste and design. This concept is really growing in popularity and makes a great talking point during the reception itself plus its deliciously fat-free on the budget front! More on this in my wedding ideas guide in the next chapter.

Hair and make-up

Again, arm yourself with a host of imagery that reflects your individual tastes and style for inspiration. Select a few luscious shots from your personal collection and add in some snaps of your favourite celebs, so you can trial a range of different looks with your hairdresser/make-up artist to see what works best. Even if you are doing your own make-up, it is a good idea to experiment with a range of looks based on the styling of your dress. Ensure you take a digi-camera along to the salon, so your hairdresser can snap your hair from different angles to give a 360degree perspective. Always add an additional 30mins onto your big day schedule as a safety measure for overall styling prep.

Stationery

I am a massive fan of personalising the big day itself and the wedding stationery is one way of getting your guests in the mood pre-event. This is also your key bit of kit to set the tone for your big day celebrations, which in turn will inspire guest outfits and their gifts. There are now masses of sites online where you and the other half can design your own invitations together... check out www.pureinvitation.co.uk

How should I word the wedding invitation?

In general, we are slightly more relaxed with our invite wording in today's Wedding World, but it is important you get all the important points across clearly and concisely whether it be relaxed or a formal ceremony. This must include: location, date and time of the wedding and reception, dress code details if relevant, a gift-list and accompanying detail on travel instructions and accomodation. Traditionally the bride-to-be's parents host the wedding and would 'request the pleasure' of the recipients company.

Is it reasonable to ask my bridesmaids to pay for their bridesmaid dresses, shoes, jewellery plus hair and make-up? Do I need to buy them a thank you present?

Personally I would always allocate a budget for the fundamental elements (such as the bridesmaids dresses)and a thank you gift is an absolute must! Again, this is all really down to personal circumstance. If the budget is limited, be upfront right from the beginning about what you can/cannot cover, so that each individual can make an informed choice as to whether they can afford to take on the role or not. In my experience people are always happy to support financially if you are clear from the beginning and give them plenty of notice to save!

How long before the wedding should you send out invitations and when should the RSVP date be?

Well I always recommend anything between 6-9months before the wedding day itself - especially if you have guests travelling from far afield or abroad. If you are working on a shorter timescale then invites need to go out ASAP. In terms of RSVP, again this depends on your individual timescale but, up to 6 weeks from the date of invite is customary.

What is the best way of asking guests for wedding gifts?

There is no need to be embarrassed about the gift list, it's a long standing tradition that people expect so be direct, it's always the best approach - you can include your gifting instructions with the wedding invite. For many this will take the form of a wedding gift list, which you can set up with the store or website of your choice. If you already have everything you need for the home, why not add in some detail about the dream honeymoon you both wish for and ask your guests to contribute to this. There are now many online sites whereby guests can log on and make direct cash donations if you prefer this option to giving banking instructions or collecting on the day itself. Again, there is no right or wrong way, just be precise in what works best for you.

What's a good running order for the day?

It's your day, so rip up the rule book and role how you want to! I hate rules!

Traditionally however, the ceremony is generally followed by photographs and then a drinks reception at your chosen venue. The wedding breakfast is next with speeches post meal, climaxing in the cutting of your cake. Finally it's time to hit the dance floor, enjoy the evenings buffet action and shed a tear over the first dance.

Usually the wedding speeches take place post meal at the reception, but there is now a new trend for presenting the speeches right at the beginning of the reception party during pre-dinner drinks on arrival. I often feel that guests are a little fresher and more attentive at this stage of the day plus it means a couple can make much more of the cake cutting ceremony post meal, which is often an area that gets overlooked.

Who should traditionally sit on the top table? (and in what order)

The bride and groom are of course centre stage and the groom should sit to the right of the bride. Next to him would normally be the bride's mother, followed by the grooms father who sits next to the chief bridesmaid. To the left of the bride would be the bride's father, who sits next to the groom's mother followed by the best man. Of course there are no rules set in stone, some people like to integrate more bridesmaids, pageboys and even ushers or close family onto the top table. And you don't necessarily have to go for a classic top table format, many couples now opt for a round table setting, which instantly gives a less formal feel to the celebration.

Who should make a speech at the reception and in what order?

Traditionally the Father of the Bride kicks off proceedings - who will note how gorgeous his daughter is looking on her wedding day, followed by the groom who should thank his new father-in-law for such kind words, before passing over to the best man for the fun bit! Quite often the bride herself will also say a few words followed by the mother-of-the-bride who can put a finishing touch on proceedings.

Tasks/responsibilities of the bestman on the day?

Besides suit hire and of course the infamous stag night pre-wedding, the best man is also responsible for organising the ushers on the day itself and for coordinating key wedding personnel to travel onwards to the reception venue (if applicable). Obviously next comes the best mans speech - oh, and we mustn't forget those all important rings during the ceremony itself! The best man is officially your right hand man so pick wisely.

How long should you allow for your professional photos?

Allow 2 weeks for digital images and then another 2-4 weeks for you final shots - ya both gonna look GORGEOUS!

Is a receiving line (bride/groom and parents meeting everyone) necessary? When should it be done?

Personally I love a receiving line as it sets a welcoming tone to the opening of your reception and for the rest of your day. This does not have to be a stiff formal line up - more a relaxed greeting at the venue just before guests sit down for the wedding breakfast.

What's the best way to stay calm on the day?

Realistically when it comes to the day itself, what more can you do? Yes, there may be a few minor dramas along the way but, it's important not to panic - simply go with the flow, soak up every second and enjoy your moment whatever happens. Embrace *your* day because this is no trial run - This is it! Allow yourself some *you* time in the morning, just to get this positive thought process on track for the whole day ahead.

Ideas for table names?

Follow your theme if applicable, alternatively you could look at favourite holiday destinations, famous landmarks or maybe hubby is a big footie fan? Table names can often provide great material for the best mans speech, especially if a few guests are linked into the story as well. Any subject matter that has a personal connection to the bride and groom always works well as an ice breaker and conversation point.

People to thank?

All those nearest and dearest to you, and of course your main crew that has made this wedding extravaganza happen... ushers, bridesmaids, pageboys, bestman, Mums and Dads etc. Remember, ones husband should also thank all your guests for sharing the day with you during his speech. Some couples also like to reference guests that could not make the day or those who are no longer with us. Traditionally the best man reads out any telegrams/messages to the couple.

*N*ext up it's time to get inspired with my mix of wedding planning ideas and top online big day destinations...

Wedding day inspiration

The proposal has been accepted, the celebratory champagne has flowed in abundance and now it's time to focus on planning your journey to the aisle of *I do*. Yes, this particular voyage is guaranteed to be the ultimate rollercoaster ride of your life and I want to make sure all your expectations are fulfilled. This day is all about you as a couple in the spotlight so, don't be afraid to stamp *your* individual style all over it. If you have a particular theme or big day vision in mind, don't hold back - this is your moment to shine. Yes, it's time to unleash your inner-beast of creative vision to ensure both the congregation and you as newlyweds walk away with a head full of sweet memories that will last a lifetime.

Of course the cake, flowers and ultimately the dress are all vital ingredients for any big day spectacular but remember, the real drama is in the detail. It's always those little extras that stand out from the crowd and make that all important lasting impression. Don't be sidetracked or deterred from integrating something a little different into the day's proceedings - make sure you plan the wedding your way. Why go for bog standard when you can make this celebration premium without necessarily breaking the bank? A stand out event is never about the amount of money spent, rather the originality and attention to detail - especially when it involves the aisle of Holy Matrimony! This day is an amazing opportunity to express individual character and ultimately your connection as a couple which no amount of money can ever buy. All you need is love as they say!

So, sit back, relax and soak up some amazing ideas to get those creative juices flowing. Anything and everything from the weird and wonderful to the classic vintage is covered for maximum drama. This inspirational mash up is all about sparking the imagination to ensure your big day is the best ever! The next few pages are all about adding those finishing touches that take any wedding from fine to fabulous in seconds. Whatever your overall theme or style and wherever your wedding is taking place, hopefully this guide of amazing ideas will hold all those hidden treasures you have been so desperately looking for. If it's memorable you want then it is memorable you shall get with a rundown of the UK's hottest list of suppliers to the wedding industry. And remember, it does not matter where you are situated across this gorgeous globe, simply take this little black book of inspiration and check out what suppliers locally can offer you. It's amazing what a little search on Google can bring up! Sometimes the best talent is literally sitting on our own doorstep...

In some cases though, we cannot fully identify exactly what it is we are searching for or actually missing from our big day plans but, that feeling of being *incomplete* rumbles annoyingly deep inside us. Indeed the wedding may be prepped to within an inch of perfection and all the essentials in place but, that does not mean everything in the garden is always rosy as they say. Maybe this gig requires that little extra something to really make it sparkle for you? Do we need to add the show into stopper and sprinkle some additional glitz into the day's glamour to truly complete proceedings? Luckily this little black book of loveliness - proudly drenched in originality, will hopefully lead you to those guarded gates of big day fulfilment and then some. Yes, it's time to ditch all those frantic attempts to find the supplier of your dreams that lead you nowhere - I have found them all for you!

Wedding planners, the time has cometh to unleash the list and get this party started!

Remember, the real drama is always in the detail

The Teardrop Shower Jewellery Bouquet by www.dcbouquets.co.uk

Big day bake off!

Talking about wedding cakes, why not take a whole new approach to this tradition with what I simply describe as *The Big Day Bake off!* Why have only 1 cake when you can have 40?! What is the idea I hear you ask? Well, when inviting ones guests to attend the biggest day of your life, why not also invite them to construct a sculpture of the sweet treat variety to bring along for your *Big Day Bake Off*. Essentially this is a competition to find the best designed, best tasting cake at the wedding, judged of course by our fresh from the aisle, utterly gorgeous - bride and groom. Oh and if you are super brave, you could also get the Mother-in-Law's involved too although, this option clearly has the potential to get very messy - quite literally! Daggers or rather top-tiers at dawn girls - I am joking of course... trust me, this is such a fun way to cut said cake and keep your guests entertained and chatting about who should have won for hours! Host a competition for adults, teenagers and children so everyone can get involved and offer a prize for the winner of each category. Ensure the presentation is properly organised with a designated host from your key wedding party to oversee proceedings. Not only is this a brilliant twist on the most classic of wedding traditions but, the *Big Day Bake Off* is also great for the big day budget too! Luckily with so many cakes being brought to the wedding, you definitely won't need to source and buy one for yourselves... let them eat on mass I say! Genius.

Wedding cake toppers

Sticking to the subject of sweet treats, I am also a massive fan of a comedy topper to add a touch of light entertainment to the cutting Ceremony. Now this could be in the form of a classic bride and groom statue or maybe in homage to a particular interest or career. My favourite collection of said toppers is available from www.cl-weddingcaketoppers.co.uk and whilst on the subject of themes, check out this hilarious scene of a newlywed couple spinning some tunes and rocking the dj booth - I wonder if they take requests?! Everything from footie fans to farming is covered with a spot of light hearted genius across the entire range of this top topper collection!

And for the first dance

Why not add a spot of showbiz showmanship to proceedings and wow your guests with a choreographed dance routine even John Travolta and the entire cast of any west end musical production would be proud of! Quite often the first dance can be a bit of a let down as the newlywed couple shift uncomfortably around the dance floor desperately trying to encourage other couples to join them. Now I rarely say no to the odd glass/bottle of champers but, in this case, an extreme intake of alcohol is never the answer to crush those pre-show nerves and let's face it, a paralytic bride with a boob popping out on the dance floor is never a good look. So, to get this show on the right road, why not check out and maybe re-create some of your fav routines from the movies online via YouTube? To help with the moves and ensure your choreography is tip top you can also turn to the professionals for support via www.firstdanceuk. co.uk. This National school of dance is available across the UK and gives couples the chance to learn a routine from the comfort of their own home thus ensuring the fox trot mash up, tango or interpretive contemporary dance is presented with confidence and conviction. Ok maybe I am taking things a little far here but, this team will defo ensure you can shape some pretty impressive moves across the floor. Talking of John Travolta, I think my first dance would have to be a remake of his classic dance-off with Uma Thurman in Pulp Fiction - legendary!

Do also remember to check out a selection of original first dances online, just type *first dance* into YouTube for all the inspiration you will ever need!

Hire an ice cream van!

All that talk of exercise has got me in the mood for an old school treat, which is exactly where www.vintagescoops.co.uk comes in! Yes, add a touch of vintage glamour and childhood nostalgia to your big day action courtesy of Betty the utterly gorgeous 50's styled ice cream van. Festooned with bunting and with Hayley the super scooper at the helm in her best floral flock, Betty and her luxurious range of sumptuous ice creams are guaranteed to be a sure-fire hit at any celebration. Infact, a vintage scoop of your favourite flavour could make a really fun alternative to the traditional pudding served at the table or possibly a welcome distraction for the little ones during the marathon photo session or reception champagne and canapés. If that doesn't tempt you, how does sticky toffee fudge or a strawberries 'n' cream sound... even better what about a champagne sorbet, baileys ice cream or pimms and lemonade? Infact screw the welcome canapés, let's all hire an ice cream instead - sweet dreams!

Confetti chaos!

For me, the confetti chucking ceremony can often be a rather messy unglamorous affair. Guests hurling handfuls of anything they can find at the newlyweds is never a good look in my book. Do we really want to see a bride half choking to death on a pink paper lucky horse shoe charm? Thankfully, it doesn't have to be like this, infact, this moment during the day's proceedings can actually be a rather spectacular, picturesque moment to capture and save for the wedding album if managed correctly. Yes, say goodbye to tack and hello gorgeous glamorous butterflies courtesy of www.ricebutterflies.com. This dream-like confetti glides through the air adding that all important touch of sophistication to this oddest of rituals. The sky will be a whirlwind of butterfly beauty as you bask in the glory of having just said *I do*. Each butterfly is actually designed to fly for 8 seconds so bask away people - I am feeling the love already! Rose petals also work really well but, for a spot of that all important extra detail slash special touch - this confetti works a treat.

Standard rice throwing is a long term tradition all over the World to bring blessings, good fortune and prosperity.

Choccywoccydoodah - A different cake altogether

Okay, so this book is really all about fine tuning those smaller details of the big day action but, I just couldn't resist throwing in a bit of choccy woccy heaven! This is the cake maker that kicks Charlie's Chocolate factory to the kerb any day of the week. Made from Belgians finest coco beans, these sculptured fantasies of gigantic proportions will add the wow factor to any big day celebration - literally leaving your guests speechless and in awe wanting more!

Yes, Choccy have everything covered for any wedding extravaganza from mouth watering statement pieces to pink lip themed lollies and even edible skull heads?! Allow yourself a moment of escape via www.choccywoccydoodah.com - quite a mouthful!

Marryoke!

Ditch the traditional wedding video and opt for something of the musical variety instead... Ladies and Gentlemen let me introduce Marryoke! This craze of the wedding pop variety has been growing steadily for some years now and gives couples the chance to cherish a montage of magical memories presented in music video format -starring your entire wedding party! We have all been in that situation where we just want to jump out the window at being forced to watch yet another wedding video that feels like it's never going to end so instead, why not opt for 5 minutes of light entertainment that totally sums up the glory of your day with a few laughs thrown in for good measure. To check out some visuals visit www.musicweddingvideos.com - the girls in this picture seem to be having a ball or maybe that's just the result of one pimms too many?!

Light introductions

Table talk can often be a little difficult at the best of times if not damn right awkward at a wedding reception - especially if the guests don't really know each other. Couples often make the fatal mistake of leaving their gathered congregation in the land of limbo, making hideous small talk whilst power drinking to ease away the pain. Before you know it, the entire wedding party is horrifically drunk hurling obscenities at each other and it's literally all downhill from there! To avoid such embarrassment altogether, why not get the guests converting over a few ice breakers to fire up the conversation?!

Start with a quiz all about... you've guessed it - our newlyweds! Each table is set the task comprising 20 questions about where you met/first date etc and then a prize of the comedy or sensible variety is issued to the winning table. On top of this you could also hold a *guess the length of the best mans speech* competition to again, encourage a bit of team play and banter per table. Erect a score board so that each team can submit a speech time with a prize for the winning group.

These simple games will unite the entire table and spark conversation leading to general comfortable chit chat. Trust me, it works every time and really relaxes the entire room into conversation just in time for those famous speeches!

DIY *cocktails!*

In homage to your new found love, why not commission and create your very own big day tipple for your wedding party to enjoy! This can often be a great alternative to pre-dinner drinks or maybe an option on the bar menu during the evening reception. A sexy name to go with said cocktail is of course essential. For some great recipes you can experiment with and tips from the best mixologists in the business visit www.thecocktaillovers.com - a classic *Sex in the City Cosmopolitan* with your own personalised twist sounds very tempting... I am breaking into a cocktail thirst just thinking about it!

Make a difference

Why not also use your special day to make an incredible difference to the lives of vulnerable children across the UK. Supporting the NSPCC's *Celebrate* scheme is quite literally the best wedding gift anyone could ever give...

There are masses of options available including personalised wedding day favours for your guests and donation cards to accompany the invites. In my experience, the originality of supporting a good cause via your wedding sets a wonderful tone and makes such a positive impact on all your guests attending before they even reach the altar! As an ambassador to this particular scheme, I know what a huge difference *Celebrate* makes to the lives of those children who really need our help. For more on this magical initiative visit www.nspcc.org.uk/celebrate

Argh! How do we get there?

In general, how dull are the pull-out set of travel instructions included in what is often a rather glamorous invite to the big day spectacular? It's always such a let down when you reach for that printed Google map of directions with local hotels highlighted in florescent marker. There must be another option out there somewhere I hear you cry? Well yes you would be right... cue www. cutemaps.co.uk! A friend of mine showed me this site and I instantly fell in love. These handmade creations are individually tailored to depict your unique journey by land, sea or air to the aisle of love and beyond! The adorable selection of imagery is vast and when it comes to getting your invitees buzzing before the big day adventure even begins - this is the kind of fun twist I am talking about. CuteMaps also offer save the date cards and even fridge magnets to remind guests of your wedding every time they reach for the butter!

Bouquet bling

This glitzy mash-up will surely have the magpies swooping over head?! When it comes to fresh ideas www.dcbouquets.co.uk are full of them in the silver, gold and very sparkly variety! Forget flowers, jewels are the future when it comes to walking down the aisle with a bouquet to die for. From Vintage to Hollywood Glamour - DC has something for all tastes and desires. I love the fact you can also integrate sentimental items of jewellery or buttons to create a truly personal *memory bouquet* - the perfect solution for carrying keepsakes from lost loved ones with you on your wedding day. The team can also incorporate *something blue* into the arrangement making the items as visible or invisible as you like. Infact you could add in the whole lot - something old, something new, something borrowed and something blue! Do all the traditions for good luck in one job lot - perfect. To check out the full gallery visit the website and drift off into bouquet heaven.

Go green

For a more sustainable invite option that is kind to the environment, why not splash your cash on something practical that won't be thrown away and more importantly can be used on a daily basis? I am of course talking about the festival-esque poster tea towels courtesy of... yes you've guessed it - www.weddingteatowels.co.uk! Get your guests in the mood for a party and give them a memento of your special day before the celebrations have even kicked off. Actually, why not go the whole hog and encourage your guests to hang said tea towel with pride in the kitchen as an homage to your special day... anything Wills 'n' Kate can do and all that!

I also love the gorgeous selection of illustrated canvas bags available via this website, ideal for creating party packs to keep the little ones entertained throughout the day or for issuing your essential detox kit for all those inevitable next day hangovers!

Take a break!

As your pre-wedding planning grows in momentum, it's important to set aside some quality time to spend with your other half to detox, de-stress and escape the W word for a few days! It's really important to organise bonding activities together that don't involve cakes, flowers, dresses and all the other wedding regalia currently occupying every spare minute of your time. In my opinion every bride and groom-to-be deserves a spot of pre-event pampering, relaxation and pure luxury so, why not go for the *Full Monty* and indulge yourselves in the wellbeing experience of a lifetime? The only problem is, once you start you simply cannot stop and will always be left wanting more... of course I am talking about the mind blowing World of tranquillity that is Champneys. Take a classic stately mansion, some elegant surrounds, add in a spot of fine dining and you have the World class facilities Champneys has to offer. This is your chance to float away to a place that takes the stress out of modern day living combined with the finest spa treatments around.

If you are both looking for an exquisite escape to realign one's inner calm and outer beauty, Champneys is most definitely the place to do it. Simply sit back, relax and enjoy the stunning scenery whilst you soak up a little Jacuzzi action open-air style. Alternatively if that doesn't necessarily float your boat as they say and you are looking for some hard core physical action, why not hit the gym to work up a sweat followed by a deep steam sauna to soothe those aching muscles, concluding with a decadent deep tissue body massage of heavenly proportions to totally unravel and relax post work-out... tempted yet?! Refresh your mind and take a moment to chillax Champneys style - a perfect excuse to treat yourself to the best stress buster in town.

I had the envious task of spending two incredible days at the Tring resort and I am not going to lie, it was all rather fabulous. Infact, the moment I landed into the grounds, I knew this gig was not going to be a hardship. The setting was quite something and that was before I even signed in at reception! Steeped in history, this elegant English mansion was opened as a health farm in 1925 by the celebrated Naturopath Stanley Lief who pioneered the concept of holistic healing. Champneys stick to those original roots today, dedicated to the wellbeing of your mind, your body and your soul.

I stepped out of the car and quite literally felt myself unwinding into a trance like state of awe and wonderment contemplating what the next few days might bring. Obviously I was not disappointed; to start with my bedroom was utterly beautiful - a classic contemporary fusion that excelled all my expectations. As ever, it's always in the detail and for sure the details at Champneys are vast - even down to supplying both fizzy and bottled water in your bedroom - how posh is that?! The minute you slip on the Champneys robe and slippers with all their magical healing powers, that's it - your hooked. I floated off for the afternoon sipping a latte whilst fingering the Sunday papers and admiring the view - total bliss.

The next day I got on-board with the philosophy, even plunging into a pool of ice cold water all in the name of wellbeing, oh and I tried out a spot of Thalassotherapy - a signature water treatment that consists of pumping a mass of healing minerals across your entire body for a total detox. Actually this particular treatment really did *detox* if you know what I mean and I felt all the better for it. Next up I was treated to a spot of blissful massage of mind blowing proportions, which definitely shifted any leftover toxins that might have been left lurking!

And when it comes to the food, well, you would be very much mistaken if you are expecting a lettuce leaf diet. The gourmet on offer was varied and delicious - a perfect accompaniment to my 48 hour inner spring clean! The principle is moderation, balance and variety but definitely not starvation. Essentially Champneys is all about creating a healthy body and mind to strengthen your overall immunity and every element of your stay will play its part. Ultimately though, it's the all inclusive, down to Earth approach that really makes Champneys so appealing and stand out from the crowd. All the staff were lovely and the treatments World class. What more could you ask for? My stay was simply faultless and I don't ever say that lightly!

So to sum up, not only is Champneys the perfect rural escape for any couple-to-be, it's also a fantastic treat for the waistband pre-wedding as well. To find out more simply visit www.champneys. com - a new healthier you is just a few clicks away.

For me, if Heaven exists - it's Champneys.

Flowers of the origami variety

I have to say, when I first discovered the work of www.thepaperflorist.
co.uk I was pretty stunned to say the least. Flowers are officially
dead - long live the paper variety I cried! Not only is this ecological
alternative to real flowers both enchanting and seriously striking,
the best part is that you can treasure them forever. The wilting days
are over people - paper is clearly the new black! Infact, having seen
this art in the flesh, there really is something about the sharp folds,
form and shape of these flowers that takes any space to a new level of
floral fantasy whatever the theme. Origami buds are so diverse and
adaptable no matter what the look - from vintage to gothic or even
high glamour. Folded flowers by The Paper Florist can also include
poems and even your own names for that extra special personalised
touch - all delivered without the worry of your favourite seasonal
bud being out of stock!

Illustrate

When it comes to getting the imagery right Ladies and Gents,
you don't get much more detailed than this little lot! Artist Sarah
Godsill has come up trumps with this ingenious way of recording
your wedding day the old fashioned way. How I hear you cry? Well,
by putting pencil to paper to create a truly beautiful collection of
timeless illustrations you can keep forever. Capturing everything
from last minute preparations, to the ceremony, reception and
the speeches, Sarah's ability to select and focus on specific details
of your big day makes her drawings a perfect accompaniment to
the traditional options of both video and photographs. Personally,
I also love the fact Sarah incorporates fragments of conversation or
phrases alongside the sketches that can often be missed but, sum up
the day's proceedings. The drawings are presented loose leaf in an
exquisite handmade portfolio and provide a unique record of your
wedding from the viewpoint of a superb artist. For more stunning
imagery visit www.eventsillustration.co.uk

The Cakes

Shoot it yourself!

A simple idea is quite often the most successful but, always the hardest to think of... why is that, it's so frustrating?! Indeed in this case, even Hilary Devey of BBC2's Dragons Den fame saw the huge commercial potential in what www.shoot-it-yourself.co.uk had to offer and decided to invest. The philosophy is very simple and the obvious clue is in the title! Yes, the wedding is filmed by your friends and then professionally edited by the team back at Shoot-It-Yourself HQ! The recording apparatus is delivered directly to your door just before the wedding and online tutorials show you what and how to film so, all you need to do is get a few mates/budding directors on board to film the action and it's as easy as that! Post wedding, the 6 hours of wobbly footage is edited down and turned into a top notch wedding video masterpiece for you and the family to enjoy. A truly unique idea that allows your guests to feel relaxed and comfortable in front of the camera due to the people they know behind it! Don't just take my word for it, check out a selection of video highlights via the website...

Blingtastic!

Cinderella eat your heart out, there is a new girl on the block and I am not talking about J-lo! For a spot of crystal slipper action of the diamante variety check out the latest offerings direct from www.rockstoriches.co.uk - total big day bling factor guaranteed! Yes, be sure to sparkle from the floor up with this ingenious idea which allows brides-in-waiting to pimp up their heels with a spot of hardcore Swarovski action. Select from a delicate coating of glitz on the heel or take it hardcore with a full body makeover. There is also an amazing selection of shoes available on the website itself so, if you haven't already picked up a pair there is no need to panic. Let the customisation commence...

DIV *Cake bake*

For those of you who REALLY want to make this gig your own, why not get a groove-on in the kitchen and whip up your very own big day super cake! The love, care and attention of this personal touch - which by the way you can shout from the rooftops on your wedding day itself, has the exact mix of ingredients to create a sweet treat of gigantic proportions for both guests and partner. Imagine the thrill of cutting one's cake knowing it was made by one's own fair hands - now that's commitment people. Perhaps this could be a team challenge undertaken by both bride and groom-to-be or maybe you could get that ever so creative friend on board who loves a spot of baking... we all have one! Whoever the chosen one will be, it's essential to learn all the top tricks of the trade when it comes to perfecting the DIY Cake bake and luckily, my friends at Squires Kitchen have all the answers and right apparatus to get down 'n' dirty with the task at hand. Come on people you can do it! Trust me peeps, the satisfaction of crafting your own bite sized slice of love is golden. Find out more about all the accessories and baking utensils you need at www.squires-shop.com and for a low down on all the World class courses and classes available to perfect your skills visit www.squires-school.co.uk. Good luck!

Candy cane

And whilst on the subject of a sweet tooth, why not get on board with the latest trend sweeping the globe and celebrate with a cascade of candy! Yes, step back Willy Wonka, when it comes to adding a touch of nostalgia and getting the guests gossiping over a few glasses of bucks fizz pre-reception www.boxcleverwedding.co.uk are the peeps to turn to. Allow your congregation to step back in time whilst digging into a retro refresher or two with this super cool old skool pick 'n' mix Candy buffet that guarantees to rock any style of celebration. And, when it comes to theming the candy buffet the World is quite literally your oyster. Take it classic or modern in terms of the sweet choices that work for you and allow the table decoration to simply follow through. I am in sweetie Heaven already!

Fun of the fair

Roll up roll up and enjoy the ride of your life! Ok maybe that was a bit extreme, but all the *fun of the fair* is a top notch solution for getting the guests on-board (quite literally) and in the mood to party. Again, when it comes to adding in a spot of big day drama it doesn't really get much bigger than this. The kids will love it and the adults will be gagging to climb on-board too! My friends at www.wantafunfair.com have all the classics including this stunning Helter Skelter plus the whizzing Waltzers, fabulous Ferris Wheel and of course you could not miss out the classic Carousel. When it comes to memorable on a massive scale - this little lot is impossible to beat. Anyone want to join me for a ride on the dodgems?!

Double take!

Ok, so to REALLY get your guests talking, this little nugget of an idea will supersede all others... on a scale of 1 to 10 how super fabulous would it be for a certain Prince William and Kate Middleton to personally rock up and welcome your guests to the Wedding Reception whilst sipping on a glass of your favourite bubbles? Well, your Wedding Fairy is all about waving that magic wand to make your dreams a reality and that includes the most famous Royals on the Planet! Cue www.alistlookalikes.co.uk - the very best in big name fakery here in the UK. Ok, so I might not be good enough to get the real thing but, at the end of the day we all love a bit of fake right?! Imagine the faces when your guests stumble across this pair -priceless! If Marilyn, Will Smith or Britney is more your cup of tea, don't worry, a-list have them covered too! Let's sprinkle some showbiz sparkle over you big day action!

Andy Williams as HRH The Duke of Cambridge alongside Jodie Bredo as HRH The Duchess of Cambridge.

News round-up

Roll up roll up and read all about it! On your wedding day there is literally only one read worth talking about and it's all about you - in the form of your very own big day newspaper. Individually designed and personalised to your own specifications, this souvenir of your wedding is the perfect way to commemorate the celebration. Share stories from childhood and teenage years, about how you met, the engagement, all the way through to the stag and hen parties and onto current day. The big day newspaper is a perfect way to keep your guests entertained during any downtime especially pre-evening party and more importantly this fabulous read is the ultimate keep sake to remember your wedding by. As I keep saying, it's all about the detail and this little treasure is truly just that! For all the low down on this unique service visit www.theweddingnews.co.uk

Table talk

Dine, sip and slice in true vintage style courtesy of the team at www.eclecticbliss.co.uk. Mix 'n' match is all the rage right now people so why not follow this sense of individuality through to the table. Uniformed identity is officially dead and that includes your crockery! There is a reason why it was known as your *Granny's Sunday Best* and that's because it was exactly that - the best my darlings! And what do we want for your wedding day... you've guessed it - the best! The Vintage theme is still going strong and if it's for you, this lovely lot of gorgeousness will definitely cement the character and charm you need to make your wedding day styling a total success. It's all about celebrating your dining experience the old fashioned way with quintessential charm, elegance and true vintage authenticity. Bring it on girls!

Sand, sun and seaside!

Let's rock this party! Whether it be as a tasty favour for your guests or just a bit of fun for the table, this traditional minty treat from the British Seaside is bound to be a total big day hit. I love the fact you can also customise by adding names, wedding date and colour ways to match individual themes. This classic nautical treat is a genius idea for any wedding - whatever the style, thanks to the team at www.the-rock-shop.co.uk. Based in the traditional town of Morecambe - British seaside rock does not come much better than this!

This way ladies and gentlemen

To the Wedding Reception of a lifetime! Yes this is serious detail people but remember, organisation is *Key* if you want your big day to go off with a bang! There is nothing more frustrating than guests going AWOL whilst dazed and confused, wondering the corridors of a wedding reception searching for the dance floor. Luckily the guys at www.shabbychicbrides.co.uk have come up trumps with a whole host of cute signage solutions to ensure your missing persons list stays blank throughout the day and night. Everything from table top signs to wine tags are covered ensuring your guests know what to do and when. Unfortunately this system may well be less effective post intake of muchos vino but hey, there are only so many miracles I can make happen with this wee wand!

Lets accessorise

Founded in 1987 by Carole Middleton, www.partypieces.co.uk is the family run business that is now recognised as the UK's leading destination for all those essential ingredients everyone needs to make any celebration seriously swing! Originally created to make event planning a little easier, PartyPieces.co.uk has everything covered for your wedding day theme - from glitz 'n' glamour to Vintage tea party. This site is my saviour for grabbing all those extra bits I always need to really bring a wedding to life. Beautiful bunting, butterfly place cards and their cup cake wraps have quite literally saved my life in the past! Defo make sure you take a moment to pop by this website and check out all the offerings for yourselves - utterly scrumptious!

Flaming Fun!

For me, a party is just not a party without a few showgirls thrown in for good measure and this lot are literally off the Richter scale. Ladies and Gents, may I take this opportunity to reveal the super spectacular talking tables - the ultimate way to serve your guests a glass of your favourite tipple they will surely never forget! These little lovelies will definitely add the wow factor at any occasion and make an exciting centrepiece for any wedding reception. Talking of wow factor, talking tables recently appeared on the x-factor so even Simon Cowell is a fan! To book the girls... or boys check out www.flamingfun.com and see what all the fuss is about! These guys also look after a whole host of other unusual acts including balloon artists, contortionists, stilt walkers and even snake charmers - all perfect alternatives for wedding day entertainment.

Smile

You're on camera! Well, in this case you are in an entire scene you showbiz Queen... get ready for the close up! Why go for the simple head shot when you can create your very own montage of movie mayhem. Ladies and Gents allow me to introduce www. wonderscene.com! This *wonderful* team have whipped up the genius idea of designing a living set, allowing all your guests to *dress up* and give a memorable pose for the camera whilst enjoying all the big day festivities. Themes include: All that Glitters, Classic Vintage, All that's British and Anything Goes - giving you the freedom to freestyle. Of course this could all get rather messy after a few light ales have flowed - especially if the guests are let loose with a dressing up box but hey, it's hilarious fun and definitely worth a few spillages here and there! Strike a pose...

Flower power

I just adore this idea that is now sweeping the UK and beyond. Forget hitting the local florist - why not take a trip down to your local flower farm instead so you can personally pick the petals you desire! No longer will you have to choose seasonal buds from a book being grown all over the globe - now a field of foliage is ready and waiting for you to explore. Yes, these floral havens are popping up all over the place and allow brides 'n' grooms -to-be the opportunity to step into a field of flower heaven to select buds together. This is seriously the stuff of a classic fairytale romance you can now live in reality! Not only that but, many farms now even offer a design service so all your floral needs can be dealt with at once, giving you the unique opportunity to personally balance all the rich colours and petal textures you have in mind for your own individual celebration and theme. The Queen of the Cut Flower Farm is Charlie Ryrie, whose estate has really built up quite a reputation for being one of the best in the business. Get inspired for your bouquets, buttonholes and beyond by visiting www.cutflowergarden.co.uk. Of course, this option is not only a wonderful experience for you both to enjoy whilst also making a really personal mark on the design of your own wedding but, it is also kind to the environment too providing a varied and sustainable alternative to mass-produced imported flowers.

Get into the groove

Talking of the latest crazes sweeping the Nation, the classic passport photo booth has to be another top alternative for getting your guests interacting whilst creating big day memories at the same time. Again, a few cheeky beers or glasses of vino helps to get your audience in the mood for mischief but, as you can see from these shots, everyone is having the time of their lives in these wedding booths with or without muchos alcohol intake and the kids absolutely love it! Infact, keeping the kids out of the dressing up box is always a task in itself, but one that is definitely worth undertaking for the fun factor. Actually who am I kidding? The adults are just as bad as the kids if not worse especially after a few naughty glasses of bubbles. Much hilarity all round and a right hoot to look back on post wedding. Check out all the detail on offer via my friends at www.groovybooth.com

A lasting memory

In my opinion the standard wedding favour can be a bit hit or miss. Most people cannot bear the sight of a classic sugared almond so why bother?! Traditionally the wedding favour is given by the bride and groom to all guests as a token of gratitude for attending the wedding and should therefore have significant meaning to you both. This gesture should - in my eyes, be a symbolic statement that represents the notion of two people coming together in marriage. For this favour to mean anything and be appreciated by your congregation, it must make an impact that stands as a lasting memory of the day. Something your guests can take away and cherish that will flourish and live on as a constant reminder of your wedding. Yes people, I am talking about a floral favour that can grow in the garden alongside your new journey together as a couple - all flowering as one! God I am SO cheesy!! Yes, private grounds across your little part of the World and beyond will be scattered with an explosion of colour in homage to your unique celebration. A truly incredible way of saying thank you to all those people who shared the day with you and more importantly, a favour that has a use and will not simply end up in the downstairs cupboard rotting until the next car boot! Trust me, your guests will also love the practicality of this gift and their garden will too! For a top selection of buds visit www.wildflower-favours.co.uk

Come fly with me!

Go up, up and away with the website that offers some truly fantastic finishing touches, covering everything from throwing confetti to the very best in venue decorations and my personal favourite of the moment - super high riding *sky lanterns*. Dating back to the 13th Century, this Chinese tradition of releasing lanterns together symbolises hope, good wishes and prosperity... a perfect finale gesture for any couple celebrating their wedding day. Once lit and released, the lanterns float gently up into the sky creating a serene scene of beauty. Gorgeously mesmerising! To order your bio-degradable lanterns in time for your big day visit www.thelastdetail. co.uk

The school fete is back!

And now you can book the whole lot for your wedding... yes, take a step back in time and reminisce about the good old care free days when the most important things in life were aiming for the coconut, successfully knocking over the tin can or splatting the rat on time! Yes the moment has cometh Ladies and Gents for those classic stalls of the school fete variety to strike back with a vengeance for your big day soiree. Obviously keeping the kids entertained during the day's festivities can often be trying at times but luckily, these little beauties will keep them going for hours! More importantly they look fabulous and will enrich any summertime celebration. Infact, they are perfect for a winter warmer too! For more information check out the offerings via my friends at www.boxcleverwedding.co.uk

Bride 2 Bride

As you well know, your Wedding Fairy loves a genius idea and this one is also up there with the very best of them! I am SO happy to have discovered www.bride2bride.co.uk. A fantastic site for brides-to-be who are looking to buy wedding dresses and all the regalia that goes with said gig at a fraction of the cost you would normally pay in a traditional bridal store. It's all in the title people - an exchange from one newlywed bride to another bride-to-be and so on and so on. It's an eco-cycle girls and I love it! Now as we all know, that dream dress you are gagging to get your hands on can cost a small fortune so it is definitely worth checking out what delights are on offer via this site. For all you know Cinderella will go to the ball and the gown you have been so desperately hunting for could be ready and waiting in the wings with your name on it! So don't delay, get online today and see what's up for grabs... let the exchange of girl power commence!

Bride2Bride

Hummingbirds

Drift off into stationery heaven with this dreamy portfolio of absolutely everything you will ever need to set the right tone for your big day celebrations. The team at www.hummingbirdcards. co.uk have created a collection of wedding day stationery that will truly captivate and excite your guests from the moment their invite arrives on the doorstep. For me, this stunning range conjures up a true mix of fairytale and romance which ultimately, is the whole point of a wedding invite that so many other stationers miss completely?! Beyond the initial RSVP, everything is covered from the orders of service to table plans, allowing you to de-stress on this often most neglected yet essential part of wedding day planning. On top of all this, the British design work behind these little stunners is second to none. Fly the flag people!

Step out in superstar style!

Always dreamt of taking a ride in a *NY Cab* or rocking up to the wedding *Grease Lightning* stylee? Well, now you can courtesy of www.starcarhire.co.uk! A theme in its own right and a real talking point for your guests, these vehicles are seriously Memorable with a Capital M and really hit the spot when it comes to Nostalgia value with IMPACT. Perhaps a trip in *Knight Riders Kit Car* is more to your liking or maybe for you *Thunderbirds* are seriously go go go! Whatever your favourite, all the cult movie cars are covered for an unusual yet fun alternative to the traditional Rolls or Classic Vintage Wedding Car. One thing's for sure, this little lot will definitely get the guests fighting over who will hitch a lift to the reception venue... severe amounts of guest jealousy guaranteed!

Bridesmaid SOS

The hunt for a selection of stand-out gowns for your girls can often be difficult if not damn right impossible. In so many cases the range of dresses on offer can be a little dated to say the least and almost certainly off-trend in terms of colour ways and cut. Why is it that the bridesmaid's gown is often so unflattering? Ok, I know we must never outshine the bride but please! Every bride I meet always seems to struggle when it comes to selecting the bridesmaid's dresses so thank God a team of UK designers thought up the fabulous World that is www.maidstomeasure.com! Panic no more girls for you can now create your very own gown allowing your bridesmaids to *work it* down the aisle of love the way you want - who needs a catwalk?! Either online or in the comfort of their studio, you select the fabrics, colour ways and style options for your wedding day look - they do the rest. Not only is MaidsToMeasure the best bespoke design service I have ever discovered, it's also much fun over a glass or two of bubbly as well... will the new Stella McCartney please stand up!

Style *SOS*

Imagine if you were able to book an *Interior Designer for Weddings* who could manage all those tiny details to exquisite perfection without the stress of having to do it all ourselves? If only I, The Wedding Fairy could magically create such a thing with the flick of my wonderful wand I hear you cry? Well my friend's, your wish is my command... allow your Wedding Fairy to introduce www.littleweddinghelper.co.uk. The panic over who is going to bring your *big day look* alive is officially over! Wedding stylists are popping up everywhere, proving to be the perfect tonic for all brides and grooms-to-be on a mission to make their overall vision in terms of look and feel of the day a reality. Maybe you just need some basic advice and support on how to integrate all those essential personal touches into the day itself or perhaps you have just discovered a dream look in a wedding magazine and want a stylist to make it happen! Wedding designers are officially my new SOS especially for integrating the finer details such as some dramatic mood lighting for romantic effect (a detail often forgotten) and for every couple out there that is struggling and frustrated by the huge task of transforming a space into their own. Let the styling commence!

Storm *of the troop variety*

May the force be with you people! Why not take things to the next level and literally land in the movie some might say is the greatest screen story ever told? Cue the *Storm Troopers* and *Mr Vader* himself... yes Ladies and Gents, the trend for *Star Wars* themed weddings is growing at quite a pace and truly puts the novel back into novelty! Imagine stepping down the aisle protected by a squad of *Storm Troopers* all standing side by side in the name of your Holy Matrimony?! Infact why not up the game and take it that one step further... for the hard core fan this could be the beginning of a full-on theme that runs throughout the entire wedding day including guest get-up! The opportunities for working with a movie concept are endless and hopefully this golden nugget of an idea may help spark the imagination for adding a quirky comedic touch to your own celebrations. Grab those *Lightsabers* and get involved peeps! One thing's for sure, the wedding breakfast menu and drinks options could be utterly hilarious - anyone for a *Chewbacca* cocktail? To book and find out more visit www.hullywoodentertainment.co.uk

Every bride deserves to sparkle

A motto I live and die by girls especially when it comes to blingtastic bridal accessories! Now for some it might be a subtle splash of glitz and for others a hard core showering of diamante? Whatever floats your boat, the team at www.libertyinlove.co.uk has a little something for every taste. From the classic tiara to a selection of show stopping contemporary head pieces - this web space has the lot! It is SO hard to find trend setting regalia to go with ones gown so thank goodness these guys have created a one-stop shop for jewellery, garters, shoes, bags and hair accessories to boot. Brands featured include Freya Rose, Peter Land and Jane Taylor Millinery all under one roof...

Power of the prop

Alice in Wonderland becomes a reality with this little treasure trove of a site I discovered recently. If you are going to theme an event you need to do it properly with a well thought selection of props and accessories to effectively bring a space to life the way you want too. I am a huge fan of popping in the odd dramatic feature or two and the team at www.eventprophire.com have come up trumps with everything you could ever possibly imagine all under one roof. This website also lists props by theme making it easy to navigate so you can focus on the pieces that fit for your wedding. From a Masked Ball to Mardi Gras, this gorgeous grotto of visual treats has something for everyone and then some!

Conjuring up something special

Talking of drama, next up is a floral feast of jaw dropping proportions! When it comes to designing with a bunch of buds, this man leads the pack. Flowers have the power to make or break a wedding and that is why I want you to check out the stunning work of Jens Jakobsen via his website www.jensjakobsen.co.uk for the ultimate in chic design - brace yourself for an explosion of perfect petals people! I purposely point out Jens work to highlight the intense level of creativity and aspiration that can be achieved through this classic art. Contemporary floral construction combines celebration and personal energy which, when done correctly can stamp stand-out originality all over the big day. Let's leave your guests spellbound...

Add the passion with a capital P

I predict an extreme temperature rise in that honeymoon suite as I write girls! It's time to take off all your clothes because it is getting hot 'n' sweaty in here and I am not surprised with this bad boy box of beauties. A health warning should be issued to your man before this little lot of luscious lingerie gets unleashed! Get St John's Ambulance on stand-by people, for Luella's Boudoir holds a super-stunning mix of delicious treats that will make any man go weak at the knees. And who could blame him? This must-view closet of satin sexiness has something for all tastes and desires to guarantee your night of perfect passion goes with a bang - quite literally! Enter the boudoir and check out for yourself by clicking www.luellasboudoir.co.uk

Gorgeous gold

As you say *I do*, slip on those bands of love in the safe knowledge that they have been made with the same tender love and care you share, not the blood sweat and tears so many gold miners sadly experience on a daily basis. The sacred wedding ring signifies the bond between you as a couple and as such, it is comforting to know they have been produced in an environment that applies ethical principles throughout. Designer Vivien Johnston launched the *Fifi Bijoux* brand back in 2006 to source fair trade gold from suppliers that make a positive impact, avoiding worker exploitation or environmental damage. The luxury jewellery business has a profound history of romance, intrigue and glamour but sadly, this has often concealed a harsher reality of cruelty, corruption and abuse. Thankfully *Fifi Bijoux* now leads the way in producing Ethically Sourced and Fair Traded wedding jewellery here in the UK, offering an incredible mix of sensational designs from the subtle simplistic to the full-on blingtastic! Be bedazzled for yourself by checking out the full online catalogue of gorgeousness... www.fifibijoux.com

The great escape

Pack your suit cases people you've pulled. Not me of course - the other half! It's time to start plotting that great escape to paradise - yes people, I am talking about the Heavenly Honeymoon! I am drifting off to the secluded sandy beaches and gin-clear waters of the Indian Ocean as we speak. After all that wedding planning you both deserve a sanctuary getaway that you will remember for a lifetime and the top team at www.turquoiseholidays.co.uk have a luxury solution for all tastes designed with passion and imagination. Covering pretty much the entire planet, Turquoise offer tailored packages from Asia to the South Pacific and beyond.

Sugary sensations!

Sweet trees are made of these and who am I to disagree? Sorry I could not resist the Eurthymics reference there! Yes the simple tree has de-barked and is now available in the sugary variety courtesy of our confectionary creators at www.sweetsensationsbyamelia.co.uk. Available in a concoction of gorgeous varieties and flavours, every sweet treat imaginable is on the menu from the retro classic to the contemporary truffle. These tasty trees of the edible variety make a great interactive alternative to the classic table centrepiece for the Wedding Breakfast or evening reception - especially when worked into an overall theme. These beauties look good enough to eat!

Kitty and ducie

Let's talk dresses! Yes, it's the vital ingredient for every girl's big day and sometimes it's just that all important budget that stands in the way of you and the dress of your dreams. And on that note, it gives me great pleasure to introduce www.kittyanddulcie.com - the website with vintage inspired gowns all under £500! Yes, you did hear me right! All the dresses are under five hundred quid and I have to say there is quite an array to choose from. From the Dolly Rocker to the Cockney Rebel and even the Bobbi Dazzler - this collection is young, fresh and incredibly sexy. Don't believe me? Just check out the website people... oh and they have just recently won best Newcomer at the Perfect Wedding Awards too!

Suited and booted

When it comes to adding a touch of superior style and sharp sophistication to the day's proceedings, ditch your man's appointment with the local hire shop from hell and get him to check-in with these 00Heaven bad boys instead...

Hugh harris

To hire a suit that sits outside the bog standard box, Hugh Harris is the only UK destination worth talking about. Working exclusively alongside iconic British tailors such as the incredible William Hunt, these guys have come up with a collection that is not only seriously smart but, also offers a design edge that distinctly stands out from the rest in the business. The collection at Hugh Harris successfully fuses traditional with contemporary design, ensuring there is something on offer for all tastes at affordable prices. Get inspired now at www.hughharris.co.uk

King and allen

Why not go for broke and take it bespoke! Yes, this wedding is a perfect excuse for him to invest in that tailored suit he has always dreamt of and more importantly actually fits! Remember some things in life are worth paying every penny for and quality cotton that doesn't instantly go up in flames if accidentally dusted in a light coating of ash during the reception fireworks display is definitely one of them! Visit www.kingandallen.co.uk for the low down on going designer on a budget - prices start from an amazing £299.

Mytuxedo.co.uk

Talking of 00Heaven, you could of course have him arrive shaken but not stirred in a super slick ensemble by the team at mytuxedo. co.uk... minus the wheels of course! Yes, quite rightly, old school glamour never falls out of fashion and always hits the hotspot at any social occasion especially a wedding day. The classic English Gent look mixed with some contemporary tailoring is bound to be a sure fire hit so why not take a tour of the website and see if anything takes your fancy: www.mytuxedo.co.uk

And finally!

Remember to check out all the latest inspirational trends and fresh styles hitting the catwalks and way beyond via your local Wedding Magazines which in the UK include the fabulous www.weddingideasmag.com, www.bridesmagazine.co.uk, www.youandyourwedding.co.uk, www.perfectweddingmag.com and www.weddingmagazine.co.uk - all amazing resources for gathering ideas to help make your big day sparkle. On top of this little lot make sure you also visit any local Wedding shows to source suppliers and add some fabulous finishing touches to your day especially www.nationalweddingshow.co.uk, www.theukweddingshows.co.uk and www.designerweddingshow.co.uk. And of course last but not least, keep up to date with the incognito 00Heaven style Queens reporting on all the coolest offerings from the wedding industry as they hit! Leading blogs include: www.rockmywedding.co.uk, www.stylemepretty.com and www.lovemydress.net - get online and get inspired...

Oh and don't forget

Before you start knocking back those deadly shots of sambuca on the hen-do, why not kick off with some hardcore get fit action to ensure you are both hot to trot and looking sharp on the dance floor. Ideally this regime should commence at least six months before the celebration itself but, whatever your timescale, every workout will make a difference and here are a couple of suggestions for optimum results...

British military fitness

Talking of hardcore, if you really want to push yourself to the absolute max and your groom has some serious anxiety issues to work off - this option is most definitely for you! British Military fitness operates 400 classes per week across the UK and all the instructors are serving or former members of the armed forces. Graded by physical ability, BMF offers an invigorating outdoor workout, which is guaranteed to leaving you buzzing by the end of your first session. As the title suggests, discipline, focus and sheer determination for the ultimate six-pack is the name of the game here! Take a trial and find out more by visiting www.britmilfit.com

Virgin Active health clubs

Live happily ever active - rather apt when you consider our subject matter! These are the words behind the brand that is the most recognised name in fitness across the UK and for good reason. Virgin Active Health Clubs offer a complete one-stop shop for both fitness and wellbeing that will take you way beyond just the wedding day itself. Ultimately if you are not already on the fitness trail, this is your chance to get on board for complete wellbeing revitalisation - you might also want to get the groom and even the bridesmaids in on the action as well. Infact, the entire wedding party could sign up to run the tread mill, take a dip in the pool or hit the Hulaerobics class on mass! Imagine how super-fit the wedding pictures would be! For more on membership and all the facilities in your area visit: www.virginactive.co.uk also available across South Africa, Italy, Spain and Portugal.

Bust that budget!

The good news is that it certainly doesn't need to cost a petrifying fortune to create a truly memorable fairytale day none of your guests will ever forget. This chapter is all about being inventive by putting your own stamp on proceedings. The very best weddings are always those soaked in personality and character so, by choosing to DIY a little - you are already half way there!

When it comes to the fundamentals of stretching your big day budget, it's always important to start local and look at what you can source on your doorstep - more importantly, you can always barter a better deal on a one to one plus you get to support an independent local trader, which is never a bad thing. Essentially I want to make sure you get a great deal and good value for money across every element of your big day. It's all about spending wisely, looking for alternatives and ultimately thinking outside the traditional wedding day box.

DIY wedding planning is most successful when we not only utilise our own talents, but also tap into all the individual skills and services our community of friends and family have to offer. Sourcing local food produce or serving traditional dishes custom to your own town or city is one instant area that springs to mind when it comes to saving cash. If it's built or grown on your doorstep, nine times out of ten it will be cheaper than shipping in from afar. Maybe a friend of a friend is an incredible chef that you can hire for all the event catering?

Always think, what can we do ourselves? Or, what can some of our close friends and family help us with? It's amazing the amount of people who know of a florist or home-baker that you could get onboard at half the standard price of a traditional supplier. And on that note, one thing to bear in mind post read... the very best way to action this hunt for local stars, is by hosting a mass brainstorm with your nearest and dearest (over a bottle or two of vino of course), to unearth said suppliers and all the budding crafters within your inner circle you may never have known about! It's always much fun with a cheeky buffet thrown in too and usually ends with a whole host of fantastic ideas coming out the other end. Book me in I am there!

So the next few pages are all about igniting that journey, by introducing you to a marvellous mix of top tips to make your wedding day truly spectacular - without breaking the bank! It's your big day so why not do it your way - all smothered in a gorgeous dollop of originality!

*L*et the budget busting DIY magic commence!

First up more on doing it all yourself

Yes if you can have a go in the home, why not have a go down the aisle as well?! Full on DIY Weddings are becoming ever more popular for truly stamping one's own mark on proceedings and maxing the big day budget. Ultimately this route is not for the faint hearted but, if you have a head for planning, are naturally creative, some time on your hands and love a challenge - this job is definitely for you!

To start with, Simply visit my *top 4 FULL ON DIY Wedding websites* for all the best tasty tips you will ever need to design and create everything from table centrepieces to DIY wedding invites plus even tutorials to do your own wedding hair updos... www.diywedding.org - www.diybride.com - www.oncewed.com and www.projectwedding.com (click ideas/diy wedding for some incredible home-grown craft solutions). Grab that sticky-back plastic girls - I am good to go!

And Whilst On The Subject Of Fabulous Online Destinations Also Check Out...

www.bridalmusings.com

Tons of fabulous out-of-the-box originality on this site for the bride-to-be who adores detail. This website is buzzing with ideas I have often never come across before - especially on the beauty and wedding favour front! Elizabeth's daily musings are above all a fun fix for us wedding- ista's, but more importantly an inspiring read for any bride-to-be. In her own words... *this is one chic and unique wedding blog!*

www.bohobride.co.uk

Fabo site for its simplicity and sexy scenic shots! Yes, I love a wee boho flick every now and then to a-light the fires for that all important photo album planning pre-wedding. Actually it's really essential to set aside some quality time on this subject matter to visualise how you would like your photographer to capture the moment in terms of look and feel of the imagery. Remember to share these thoughts/concepts directly with your photographer to ensure you are both singing from the same hymn sheet as they say! In my experience, all good suppliers are very happy to receive such detailed information so they can interpret into their own style and bring the big day vision alive. *Natural is the name of the game here at Boho Bride and I love it.* Let's go create some memories together gorgeous wedding planners...

www.omgimgettingmarried.com

It's all about the drama at destination OMG! Yes, if it's glitz, glamour and all-round general gorgeousness you are on the hunt for - this is the Mother of all Mecca's. The site is SO brilliantly easy to navigate, plus the pages have been cleverly categorised meaning you can access the elements you are researching quickly and effectively - no trolling through hundreds of pages here people! Pay special attention to the video reels for some pretty impressive visuals that have been carefully selected by the sites editor to inform and spark the imagination. Throw in select reviews on the latest bridal-wear launches, crazy cool cakes, fabulous flowers, a handful of seriously stunning stand-out venues and all of a sudden OMG becomes an essential click for any fashionista bride-to-be!

www.thebridescafe.com

Sophistication is the name of the game at this establishment, mixed with a side order of dreamy elegance. If you are looking for some edgy designs that are fresh, contemporary yet still fairytale - you need to head over to this cafe post haste! Forget the cake and cappuccino; this is one of the very best comprehensive online blogs I have ever come across. Literally everything is covered from your stationery to the ceremony and all that happens in-between!

www.bridalbeautybuzz.com

My number one online destination for lippy, liner and everything in-between! Award winning make-up artist Sarah Brock has come up trumps with this leading blog reviewing all the major brands, alongside a whole host of newbie's and independent beauty ranges for every possible skin complexion. Whether you are having your make-up done professionally or applying yourself, there is much to learn from this leading lady of bridal beauty. I love all the practical advice and wide mix of looks from L'eau natural to full on red carpet glitz - time to experiment girls!

www.theperfectpalette.com

Planning the overall colour scheme for your wedding can often be a time consuming and stressful process especially when you have no clue where to start! Luckily the team behind this site have prepped up a comprehensive guide to mixing colour-ways, covering everything from the bold and beautiful, to the delicate and subtle, meaning there is a wide range of styles and themes that will work across all seasons at any wedding. Bring on the mood boards *en masse!*

www.offbeatbride.com

Again, this one does exactly what is says on the tin! If the classic Cinderella fairytale is not for you, head on over to 'offbeat' for a sexy selection of wedding day alternatives. This is the blog that promises to *altar your thinking* and I must say - it ticks every box for me! Don't be afraid to click on the *wedding porn* pages - they are far from seedy, trust me! Oh and if you are bored of the classic tiara and twin pearls set, this website has some really cracking fashion accessories to explore.

www.hdofblog.com

Hair up or hair down - what is a bride-to-be to do?! Well, first up, look no further than this fabulous follicle bible I am always logging on to for inspiration. Whether it's long, short, thick or thin, the team at *hair dressers on fire* have a little something for everyone - I am talking about the hair here people! This website could not be any more bang on-trend if it wanted to, uncovering all the latest fixes from the fashion World as and when they happen. Make sure you also check out the tutorials page so you can have a go at an 'updo' yourself... get ready for the shampoo and set girlies!

www.thebrokeassbride.com

Bad-ass inspiration on a broke-ass budget - what a hook-line! Yes, this website does exactly what is says on the tin and it's a total must-see for maximising cash and making the most of your big day budget. We are talking from fine to fabulous in seconds wedding planners - without having to break the bank! Head straight over to the categories page for a brilliant breakdown on how to spend wisely and effectively across each element of your big day. Remember a fairytale does not have to cost the earth people - it's all about what you know not who you know!

www.bride2bride.co.uk
(in the US check out www.MyBridalBids.com)

As you well know, your Wedding Fairy loves a genius idea and this one is right up there with the very best of them! I am SO happy to have discovered www.bride2bride.co.uk. A fantastic site for brides-to-be who are looking to buy a wedding dress and all the regalia that goes with said gig at a fraction of the cost you would normally pay in a traditional bridal store. The detail is all in the title people - an exchange from one newlywed bride to another bride-to-be and so on and so on. It's an eco-cycle girls and I love it! Quite often that dream dress you have been gagging to get your hands on can cost a small fortune, so it is definitely worth checking out what delights are on offer via this site. Don't delay, it turns out Cinderella will go to the ball! Get online today and see what's up for grabs... let the exchange of girl power commence!

www.whimsicalwonderlandweddings.com

When it comes to soaking up a few ideas for theming your wedding - this site is loaded with a sensational spectrum of ideas. The imagery is seriously hot and the contributors even hotter! In particular, this website offers a stunning mix of really fresh wedding photography portfolios to tickle your taste buds and inspire your own big day celebration. *The Bride Diaries* are also a must-read for any bride-to-be... you are not alone Ladies!

www.polkadotbride.com

Buckets of wedding wisdom here at Polka Dot Bride especially when it comes to the key elements of your big day. The floral offerings are particularly spectacular as are the inspirational interiors. I also love the *groom's page* which offers a male perspective on the crazy World that is *Weddings* - take note girls!

Quick fix budget and diy solutions!

*R*ight first up, discuss openly with immediate family who will be contributing to the wedding - it's important to sort such technicalities out at the very beginning of this process. If you feel uncomfortable asking a direct question, initially mention the budget as a passing comment to sow the seed as they say... that is if they don't mention it first! Tact and diplomacy is the name of the game here. It is also important to be understanding of individual financial circumstances.

And before you even think about starting the planning process, remember to host a house party for the engagement if you haven't celebrated already... everyone will bring a bottle and hopefully a present too! I am packing an overnight bag as we speak!

Let's start with the venue

Why not hire a village hall and bling it up yourselves! In-fact take any space that can be decked out DIY stylee, as this will always be the cheaper option. Local farmers often have rustic barns that can be transformed for a summer wedding, or you could even host your nuptials in your own back garden! If you or someone close to you has a large outdoor space, it would be wise to look at hiring a marquee and again decking out yourself. This option is always a sure fire hit in my experience and generally makes for an unforgettable wedding. Outdoor catering is often much cheaper than a venue alternative, although if you are feeling super brave, you could always go buffet style and prep everything in advance yourselves with a

DIY catering team. Get Mum's, Dad's and the In-law's on board and transform into a pre-wedding bonding session. And in terms of serving on the day, why not ask any friends with older teenagers to take on the role of waiters/waitresses... great work experience for sure! From this point, you can follow through with a DIY bar situation and literally save thousands on hospitality fees. In some cases a temporary event notice is needed in the UK to serve alcohol if being charged for at the event - simply check and apply with your local authority. Again, wherever you are located in the World, it is always best to check legal provisions in place for serving alcohol and providing live entertainment in either a public or private place.

If you are keen on a more traditional venue, consider opting for a weekday celebration as this option is always much lighter on the budget and if you give guests notice, they should be able to plan around work commitments. In some cases you can knock up to 50% off venue and catering costs. Also don't forget to look at intimate local restaurants you may be able to hire for the evening, which again are always lighter on the budget - especially if booking a week night celebration.

And finally, some of the National hotel chains such as the Holiday Inn, are now offering wedding packages all in for just 1k including buffet, entertainment, red carpet arrival and all the general big day regalia! What a steal!

Wedding planning details

When it comes to the photographs, do you have a confident friend or family member who might be a keen amateur you can hire? Simply make a list in advance of all the shots you require in classic form (i.e. portraits of key wedding party members/group shots etc) and you are good to go! Oh and make sure they also freestyle with a bit of reportage photography, just so they also capture all those unexpected moments too. Whilst on the subject of photography, wedding day illustrations are also a gorgeous and unique way of capturing the magical moments of your big day that you can hang on your walls and treasure forever.

Again with the dress, hunt out a local independent designer who can put a bespoke number together for you at half the price of a classic bridal store. I don't suppose there is a gorgeous vintage styled wedding dress that can be passed down and altered for a contemporary bride? Talking of family heirlooms, what about a wedding ring that might be passed across to the next generation?

And when it comes to shoes, accessories, veils and tiaras you really cannot beat www.etsy.com/weddings for an amazing selection of new and vintage themed designs. I especially LOVE the glitzy array of shoe clips on offer, meaning you can jazz up a standard pair of heels from the high street at half the price! The DIY department is also fantastic for adding those all important finishing touches to every element of your big day, from wedding favours to table centre pieces. Oh and for sexy bridal lingerie that won't break the bank, check out www.debenhams.com/lingerie - there are often great deals to be had online! And on the hair and make-up front, you could also go DIY with the support of your maid of honour. Remember practice makes perfect!

Ok onto transport, forget hiring a V expensive vintage car - someone you know must have a super snazzy set of wheels you can use to arrive in style? Talking of the ceremony, for a cheap yet glamorous alternative to the traditional confetti affair, simply grab some pink tissue paper, make a heart template and cut out en masse for your congregation to toss once the deal is sealed as they say! Even better, these little hearts of love would also be perfect for your little flower girl to scatter as you walk down the aisle to say I do. So cute!

On the ceremony entertainment front, ditch the harpist and hunt out a local emerging talent to play acoustic guitar - if they can sing or know a singer that would be wonderful too! In-fact, they may be part of a full 4-piece band that can play in the evening as well! Local entertainers such as jugglers, caricaturists and magicians are also wonderful touches for the reception pre-dinner drinks and are usually 15% cheaper when booked directly and not via an agency. And on that note, ditch the classic DJ and go for an iPod wedding instead! Yes, iTunes have launched an app for organising your own big day playlist and evening's entertainment. Check out MyWeddingDJ via the iTunes store for more detail.

Talking of the dance floor - make your own entertainment by choreographing the first dance to your favourite track of movie theme... check out YouTube for some serious high kick inspiration! Just type first dances. You could also make your own wedding music video - get everyone on the dance floor, play your favourite track and let the magic happen! If you have a smart-phone you could even edit it together like a pro too! Hosting a pub quiz as part of the day's activities or indeed during any downtime between reception and evening-do is also a fabulous way to keep all your guests entertained.

Right, next up let's move onto the gift list! My first bit of advice is to not be afraid of adding all those top-end items you have been dreaming of. Ok a Ferrari might be pushing it but, if you are setting up home and need a washing machine - why not give it a whirl?! Of course, if you are already all set and good to go with the love nest, you might be looking for guests to contribute to the honeymoon? Well if that is the case, why not check-out www.honeymoonpixie. com and set up a honeymoon gift registry, so all your guests can start giving today! It's really easy to activate an account and you can notify all your friends and family of the gift-list by facebook or email, which also includes a cute announcement card. This option is SO much more glamorous than simply asking for peeps to pop a little something into your account... I can taste that minty mohito already!! On a serious note though, if you do feel uncomfortable asking for cash, just make a joke of the situation i.e. we have the toaster and tea towels, so we are keen to head off to Thailand instead!

Oh and when it comes to giving gifts to your key wedding party personnel, why not go DIY on this task as well. Ok, you have the classic jar of strawberry jam that could be a possibility, but what about brewing your own batch of wedding day wine, that could also be served during the wedding reception as well?! For me, this is beyond gorge - the best personal touch ever for your big day celebrations and more importantly - fantastic on the budget side of things too. More on DIY winemaking in a minute, but in the meantime, if you also fancy adding something a little bit different to proceedings, why not head over to www.nutbrookbrewery.com to brew your very own British beer! I am defo down for a pint!

More on the reception

Put a shout out for any budding carpenters! Sign them up to produce your personalised wedding day signs/arrows directing guests to the reception. Fingers crossed you may be able to get your hands on a professional, in which case the possibilities are endless!

Candy stalls are all the rage at big day do's right now and SO easy to put together yourself. Visit www.weluvsweets.com to sample a fabulous mix of American retro and classic English sugary treats for your guests to enjoy and reminisce about the good ole days! Grab yourself a red and white striped (candy styled) tablecloth, a few glass jars and you are good to go! Parental supervision of children accessing said sweets is highly advised!!

On that note, what about a few traditional fete stalls to keep the little ones entertained during pre-dinner drinks? I love a bit of splat the rat or a classic coconut shy to get the guests going and don't even get me started on a hook the duck competition! This option is V easy to put together yourselves... a paddling pool, a few yellow ducks, some canes, bang in some hooks and a couple of fun prizes to win - you are good to go! These games work especially well within a vintage themed celebration, or when the wedding reception is being hosted in a marquee with direct outside space you can dress-up.

And whilst on the subject of keeping the little ones entertained, sweet treats don't come much better than these retro wonders - www.lovehearts.com... they have some wonderful options for your wedding favours too! Oh and thinking of edible wedding favours, why not have a go at making those as well! Check out www.cakeypigg.com for a selection of courses you can join to learn everything you need to know, or integrate into your hen party.

The costs involved with hiring chair covers is a massive bug bear of mine so why bother?! Just do your own covers instead. Quite often a simple chiffon bow tied around the back of a chair can produce the desired effect or, you could try negotiating (with your venue) the supply of chairs that work well within the space and do not necessarily need covering. It might also be an idea to ditch the classic floral centrepiece! For starters you could opt for sweet trees which look stunning on the table and taste even better - much fun for getting your guests talking - www.sweettreefactory.co.uk! Dramatic candelabras work well for a spot of table drama and make a perfect base to accessorise around. Candles in general are always great for creating a romantic ambience - especially for a winter wedding or evening reception. To keep on top of your budget, check out local second hand stores for gothic candelabras and general vintage regalia/tabletop pieces that you can mix-in with your theme. In-fact, a good rummage at your local car boot sales and charity shops is always recommended - you never know what you might find that could work-in with your overall styling. Printed black and white photos of you both popped in vintage frames as part of your centrepiece is also a really lovely touch.

Bunting and balloonage in general is never a bad thing, especially in the right setting - think village hall/classic rural retreat... remember balloons are fabulous for adding height to your tables.

If you are still keen on a bit of classic floral action, you could opt for a simply styled yet eye-catching display, by gathering all the necessary display props and getting a best pal on board to put everything together for you on the wedding day itself. Retro tea-pots, jam jars and water jugs work so well when grouped together as a central table piece - especially for a vintage celebration, filled with an abundance of floral treats. If going monochrome for example, simply gather an eclectic mix of black & white vases and select the buds to coordinate accordingly and so on. Contemporary silk flowers have also come on leaps and bounds in terms of styling over the last couple of years and make a great option for prepping in advance - especially pew ends and centrepieces... www.dunelm-mill.com have a wonderful selection. Remember if you can't find what you are looking for in general and are stuck for sourcing stuff, hit Ebay or Etsy for guestbook's, cake stands, candelabras and plates etc.

PLEASE also check out this amaze site www.save-on-crafts.com/bridalveilshop.html - based in the USA, these guys have the best ideas for doing it yourself from spraying tree branches gold to using bird cages as your table centrepieces! A total must see for inspiring you big day...

Oh and one more thing re the venue, sprinkle lavender seeds in the reception area to give your guests a warming welcome on arrival!

Food glorious food

To make your budget go further, why not opt for a 2 course menu (a hearty mains and pudding) instead of the classic three course dinner. If you are serving a few pre-reception canapés or nibbles with drinks, then this can act as a starter. In-fact most people are usually fit to burst by the time it gets to enjoy the pudding anyway! Another option would be to opt for a starter and main course and then serve your cake as a pudding - thus getting all three courses in. On the other hand, you could be clever with your timings and host a later wedding ceremony, so you only have to serve a wedding breakfast and not an evening buffet as well.

Remember to always focus on local specialities as these often work out to be much cheaper. Think of your location. If near Cheddar for example, why not serve mini Hors D'oeuvres of cheddar cheese chunks with a dollop of pickle on mini crackers during pre-dinner drinks... or mini Cornish pasties if you are based in Cornwall? A delicious Lancashire hotpot would also go down a treat as a main course too! You get my drift right?! A hog roast or big bowls of fresh pasta make a great alternative to the traditional evening buffet and are much lighter on the budget too. Beware of evening buffets as they can often work out to be very costly. Themed foods such as platters of Indian or Chinese dishes can also work out to be more cost effective and make a fun, memorable alternative to classic wedding day cuisine. Following on from this point, your entire wedding day look could be inspired by the menu you choose. If going Oriental, think about how you can run this theme across the entire celebration. Mexican cuisine is also really popular at the moment as is tapas, which is particular good for getting your guests interacting and talking at the table. Sharing food is always V sociable and perfect for a wedding.

Another option would be to pick your favourite three courses as a couple and start planning your wedding food from that point. If burger and fries washed down with a sweet sundae is your thing, then maybe Fifties American retro could be your running theme! And so on... remember though, whatever you decide on, always steer well clear of luxury foods and posh fish to keep the costs down!

Serve prosecco or cava for the toasts instead of Champagne, no-one will ever know the difference and prosecco in particular, generally tastes much nicer that the average bottle of bubbly anyhow. Of course, you could totally ditch the Champagne altogether and go for a DIY cocktail instead for a pre-reception drink ... this alternative is always very light on the budget front - especially when utilising minimal alcohol content!

And for the hardcore, why not go down the Homemade wine route - a perfect option if hosting your big day in a DIY space, or maybe you can simply negotiate a basic corkage rate in a more traditional venue... now we are talking personalisation people! Take a look at www.wineworks.co.uk for inspiration - my Dad made a batch of Red from this site and it tasted gorge!

Don't feel obliged offer a free bar - ½ a bottle of wine per person plus one DIY cocktail is sufficient... oh and don't forget a few bottles of beers for the boys too! Most wedding guests do not expect a paid-for bar anymore.

If you are not sweet toothed, go for three tiers of savoury cheese instead and serve with crackers, biscuits and pickle - this option is often much lighter on the budget and makes a refreshing change for your guests... visit www.thecheeseshed.com

And talking of wedding cakes, don't forget to always go for a sponge based filling if opting for the traditional sweet treat route (flavoured if you fancy), as this option is always much cheaper than going all fruity!

And for a show-stopping spot of glitz at the table - why not wow your guests by adding in some edible flowers to your main dish of the day! V cheap and V fabulous visit www.maddocksfarmorganics. co.uk for visuals.

Onto the last important bits

*D*iscuss potential ideas or things you would like to do for the stag and hen parties with your maid of honor and best man. Visit www.gohen.co.uk and www.gostag.co.uk for some serious inspiration!

Book wedding insurance... get the low-down via www.moneysupermarket.com/wedding-insurance

Consider putting together a fun wedding website to keep guests up-to-date with your plans, or create a Facebook page to stay in touch. Visit www.mywedding.com/free-wedding-websites for ideas.

And finally, don't dismiss a wedding abroad - your cash can often stretch much further than a classic bash in the UK!

www.weddings-abroad-guide.com

I refer to this site all the time when it comes to the legalities and technicalities of getting hitched abroad. And when it comes to sourcing suppliers and tour operators, this website also has a great mix of solutions. I particularly love all the really practical advice offered to couples, in terms of making sure the wedding is legal and ensuring the wedding documents are officiated at your local registry office when you return home. A really easy-to-use self help guide that is a total must see if you are marrying abroad.

The final word

I have said it before, but I will say it again!

Don't forget to book locally and rally all your friends and family to get onboard and support with the planning process right from the off. Someone will know someone who does hair, or works as a DJ on the weekends or indeed has a proper posh car they can loan you... even better offer as a wedding day gift! I am always amazed at how much can be achieved in planning a wedding with the resources right on our own doorstep and no matter where you are located in the World, I hope this book has given you a few ideas to hunt them out... now is the time to also utilise Google for finding local suppliers! If you want to be super brave, why not have a go at some of the elements yourselves? Some local colleges offer a whole spectrum of courses, from cake making to flower arranging that you could try out.

Ok, next up it's the budget, remember to work out how much cash you have to splash and take out 10% for emergencies. Steer clear of mentioning the 'W' word wherever possible - this is much easier when thinking DIY and planning elements yourself. In some cases the 'W' word can double your costs as suppliers try to cash in on your celebrations - so be cautious. On top of breaking down your budget, remember to also make a check list of what you need to be doing and when with your very own *big day planner...* especially important if going DIY - one needs to be super duper organised!

And finally - *Negotiate And Barter Every Step Of The Way.* As I always say, most wedding services are on a local level, so start by offering a little under the cash amount you have pre-allocated and see what the provider can offer. Wouldn't it be amazing to come in under budget!

Right people my work here is done! Magic wand waved and fairy-dust officially sprinkled! It's time for your Wedding Fairy to sign off and leave you to get on with planning the most sensational day of your life. I do truly hope this guide has not only inspired, but also given you a base outline to start working from in terms of planning the day itself.

Your very own journey to the aisle of 'I do' start's right here...

Make sure you enjoy every second